FEDERAL TRANSFERS AND INTER-STATE DISPARITIES IN INDIA

J.R. GUPTA
MANJIT KALRA

ATLANTIC
PUBLISHERS & DISTRIBUTORS

Published by

ATLANTIC
PUBLISHERS & DISTRIBUTORS
B-2, Vishal Enclave, Opp. Rajouri Garden,
New Delhi-110027
Phones : 25413460, 25429987, 25466842

Sales Office
7/22, Ansari Road, Darya Ganj,
New Delhi-110002
Phones : 23273880, 23275880, 23280451
Fax : 91-11-23285873
web : www.atlanticbooks.com
e-mail : info@atlanticbooks.com

ISBN 81-269-0420-8

Printed in India
at Nice Printing Press, Delhi

ACKNOWLEDGEMENTS

We gratefully acknowledge the valuable guidance and immense help rendered to us by Mr. Tejindar Singh Kalra, Principal Chief Electrical Engineer, Central Organisation Railway Electrification, Allahabad, without which we would not have been able to accomplish this study. We shall ever remain indebted to him for his kind and selfless cooperation. We extend our sincere thanks to Mrs. Bimla Gupta who provided the much needed moral support and encouragement which enabled us to concentrate on this work.

We also place on record our thanks to Mr. Pankaj Sharma, Dy CEE/ CORE, for his valuable assistance in composing the book and to Mr. Rupesh Kumar Suman for efficiently carrying out the computer work of several drafts of this book. Last but not the least we are grateful to Atlantic Publishers and Distributors for publishing this book in a record time.

J.R. Gutpa
Manjit Kalra

PREFACE

The present study is an attempt to evaluate the role of four main channels of Federal transfers (Finance Commission, Planning Commission, Central Ministries and Financial Institutions) in reducing the persisting inter-state disparities in India. The Federal transfers must be in accordance with fiscal needs and fiscal capacities of the States, the estimates of which are also the subject matter of this book. It also aims to evaluate the role of State Governments in mobilizing their own resources and thereby providing basic socio-economic services to their residents. The book comprises seven chapters with sections and sub-sections wherever required.

The first Chapter is an introductory Chapter to make the reader aware of the growing and persisting inter-state disparities in India. It is important to first present the problem and then go into the reasons responsible for existing disparities and then formulate corrective measures needed to reduce the inter-state disparities to a functional, desirable and acceptable level. This Chapter is divided into three sections. Section one presents the persisting and widening inter-state disparities. Section two brings out the reasons for inter-state disparities in India through a review of literature on the issue. Section three relates to the statistical tools used and methodology applied in computing the composite index of development, fiscal capacity and fiscal needs of the States.

In the second Chapter floor-fixing of required level of services is done and minimum per capita expenditure required to provide such services in States is estimated. In this context the Chapter is divided into four sections. In Section one a relative composite index of development is prepared by selecting 18 socio-economic indicators of development reflecting the existing level of services in different States. A review of choice of indicators in various studies is also discussed. Section one is further sub-divided into four parts :

A. Selection of indicators of development.

B. Physical Quality of Life Index (PQLI) applied to indexing of physical values of indicators.

C. Absolute and relative performance of States by PQLI.

D. Performance of States on the basis of PQLI 1991 over 1971.

In the second Section fixation of minimum level of required services which all States must at least provide to their resident in a federal set-up is computed . Also the optimum level of services which all States must strive for is presented. The optimum level of services is the one existing in the best performance State (PQLI=100). In the third Section a Need Table is computed by computing the difference between the existing level of services (what is) and required level of services (what ought to be). In the fourth Section per capita and total additional expenditure required to provide the needed services in which the States are below the required level of services is computed. It is the per capita expenditure required in the short run to cover the gap between the existing and required level of services which must be ensured to the States through the transfer of resources from the Union . Also, the additional expenditure required to achieve the optimum level of services in the long run is presented.

The third Chapter discusses the unequal fiscal capacities of States. States do not have equal fiscal capacities; therefore, the transfer of financial resources has to be, deliberately and consciously, much greater to backward fiscal disadvantaged states. Horizontal fiscal balance implies the existence of some form of revenue sharing arrangements or equalization grants to remove the inequalities in fiscal capacity, provided that the States mobilize their own resources at a comparable standard of their fiscal capacity. In this context the Chapter is divided into three sections. In the first Section the methodology for computing fiscal capacity of States is discussed. In the second Section computation of fiscal capacity is done in four steps :

A. Essential Consumption

B. Gross and Net Economic Surplus

C. Private Investment

D. Fiscal Capacity—Absolute and Relative

In the third Section tax efforts of States are discussed. Before deciding on the pattern of restructuring of federal mechanism of transfer of financial resources to States, the tax efforts of States in accordance with their relative taxable capacity must be viewed.

The fourth Chapter is meant to evaluate the role of Finance Commissions in reducing the inter-state disparities. In this context the Chapter is divided into four sections. In the first Section the role of first Eight Finance Commissions, covering a period from 1952-53 to 1988-89, is discussed. This period is termed as gap filling approach of Finance Commissions. In the second Section the role of instruments of fiscal equalisation in reducing the inter-state disparities *viz.*, taxes and grant-in-aid is brought forth. In the third Section the role of the Ninth and Tenth Finance Commission covering a period from 1989-90 to 1999-2000 is discussed. This period is termed as the Normative Approach of Finance Commissions. In the fourth Section a note on the Eleventh Finance Commission is presented.

The fifth Chapter examines the role of plan assistance from the Planning Commission and discretionary grants from the Central Ministries to the States under Article 282 of the Constitution. Plan assistance will cover both: the grants under Article 282 and loans under Article 293 of the Constitution. In this context the Chapter is divided into two sections. In the first Section the role of the Planning Commission from 1951-52 to 1989-90 is examined. In the second Section the role of Central Ministries is discussed.

In the sixth Chapter the role of commercial banks and all India financial institutions is examined in the context of reduction in inter-state disparities. Commercial banks and financial institutions can play a dominant role in promoting balanced development of the country, acting as agencies mobilizing a substantial portion of the community's savings. Correction of inter-state disparities in banking development was one of the major objectives of nationalising the fourteen major commercial banks in July, 1969. With the nationalisation of the major banks and creation of public financial institutions, a large segment of the non-budgetary resources of the community came under the control of the Union Government. The allocation of non-budgetary resources to the States must also satisfy the norm of reduction in inter-state disparities.

The seventh Chapter draws out the conclusions in two Sections. In the first Section the criteria adopted by different agencies are evaluated. In the second Section conclusions of the study are presented. Economic backwardness is a self-feeding process. A backward State in a backward country like India has a double disability. The economic backwardness of the country and that of the State interact and reinforce one another. A large proportion of population in these States lives under conditions that are unsatisfactory as compared to those prevailing elsewhere in India—conditions which can be defined sub-human in absolute terms. A State may be poor or rich, backward or advanced, underdeveloped or developed, in absolute terms, but its backwardness is relative to other States' development. Thus, the inter-state disparity can be reduced only when the financial transfers from the Finance Commission, the Planning Commission and Central Ministries and also by the Financial Institutions are in accordance with the relative fiscal capacities of the States and their relative fiscal needs as indicated by the relative composite index of development. So far these financial transfers have not been able to make any dent on inter-state disparities. By and large the backward States have been found to be making adequate efforts to mobilize their own resources through taxation.

J.R. Gutpa
Manjit Kalra

CONTENTS

LIST OF TABLES

LIST OF APPENDICES

1

INTRODUCTION

Ever since Independence, the issue of inequalities in the level of development of various States has agitated economists, policy makers and of course the people of the backward States. Talking to the people in Bihar, Madhya Pradesh or Orissa, one realizes that they consider, Punjab or Haryana, similarly the way Punjabis or Haryanvis think of Japan and United States. This by itself shows the extent of economic disparities within the nation. It becomes obvious to anyone traveling by a bus or train from west to east, or north to south that India remains a land of contrasts. As one starts from Amritsar on a journey to Calcutta, one notices how the people of Punjab are much healthier, better dressed and obviously wealthier than those of Uttar Pradesh and Bihar. Similarly traveling from Delhi to Bombay or to Gujarat one realizes how with a change of landscape and state boundaries one comes across miles and miles of sand-dunes and 'wilting' crops in Rajasthan, uneven terrain in Madhya Pradesh with narrow roads winding through forests, pock marked mining towns, tribals huddled together on railway platforms and bus stands and jawar-bazra and oilseed crops struggling to survive without irrigation.

At the outset problem of inter-state disparities, its magnitude and pattern has to be spelt out, before the role of multi-agencies, *i.e.*, Finance Commission, the Planning Commission, and All India Financial Institutions can be examined and judged in reducing the inter-state disparities in the levels of development.

It is important to first present the problem, the reasons responsible for existing disparities and the corrective measures needed to reduce inter-state disparities to a functional, desirable and acceptable level. In this context this chapter has been divided into three sections :

Section 1 - Presents persisting and widening inter-state disparities.

Section 2 - Brings out the reasons of inter-state disparities in India.

Section 3 - Presents stastical tools used and methodology applied.

SECTION 1 - PERSISTING AND WIDIENING INTER-STATE DISPARITIES IN INDIA

Everyone living anywhere in India is entitled to equity in respect of facilities like roads, electrification, health and education by the very fact of being a citizen of this democracy. The development of these facilities is a matter of national commitment. The traditional 'trickle down' theory of development has failed to automatically solve the problem of backward States. The poorer States have not developed much despite considerable growth in the national economy.

Table 1.1 shows the average indices of per capita income of the States since 1960-61. Indices have been worked out by taking the average per capita income of the States (in different years) as 100.

In 1960-61 the below average States happened to be Karnataka, Rajasthan, Andhra Pradesh, Madhya Pradesh, Kerala, Uttar Pradesh, Orissa and Bihar. Similarly, the indices for different States based on their average per capita income in 1970-71, 1980-81, 1990-91, 1996-97 have been computed in Table 1.1. The analysis of table 1.1 brings out the following trends :

- The deceleration in Punjab and Tamil Nadu was from relatively higher levels of per capita income. Punjab the richest state had per capita State Domestic Product twice that of Bihar in 1960-61.
- The acceleration is particularly marked in Maharashtra from 1990s. Gujarat has shown continuous acceleration since 1960s. It has retained its high level status.

- Per capita income in 1990-91 and average per capita income index in 1990-91 through 1992-1993 reflect a similar trend — only four States Gujarat, Haryana, Maharashtra and Punjab are above average index States. Tamil Nadu having an above average index (111) in 1960-61 had only 92 average per capita income index in both the time periods 1990-91 and 1990-91 through 1992-93.

Table 1.1

Average Indices of States According to Their Per Capita Income

States	1960-61	1970-71	1980-81	1990-91	1990-91 through 1992-93 Average	1996-97
1	2	3	4	5	6	7
Gujarat	120	115	127	117	118	136
Haryana		134	147	150	154	150
Maharashtra	136H	117	140	152	160	162
Punjab	122	173H	180H	168H	172H	165H
Tamil Nadu	111	93	87	92	92	107
West Bengal	130	109	93	96	92	88
Andhra Pradesh	91	87	94	94	88	94
Karnataka	98	92	93	92	95	96
Kerala	86	92	82	80	80	94
Bihar	71L	58L	57L	53L	53L	39L
Madhya Pradesh	86	80	70	70	74	69
Orissa	72	80	74	72	73	54
Rajasthan	94	80	81	81	80	82
Uttar Pradesh	84	84	73	71	73	61
Coefficient of Range	0.31	0.50	0.52	0.52	0.74	0.62

Source : Computed on the basis of Appendix 1.1

Note : Haryana did not exist in 1960-61 (therefore there are only 13 States)

Coefficient of Range = $\frac{H-L}{H+L}$ Where H stands for the highest and L for the lowest.

Inter-state disparities have widened and persisted over-time. Punjab's per capita income is now four times that of

Bihar. The unstated assumption that inter-state disparities would narrow with national development has failed. The pattern of development reflected in table 1.1 shows that backward States have been left further behind the developed States. West Bengal, Karnataka, Bihar, Madhya Pradesh, Orissa, Rajasthan and Uttar Pradesh, reflect a continuous a decline in average per capita index. West Bengal happened to be a above average State in 1960-61.

- Andhra Pradesh and Kerala are the only two below average State which have improved their average per capita index during the time period 1960-61 to 1996-97.
- India today nearly after five decades of Independence has only five States (Punjab, Maharashtra, Haryana, Gujarat and Tamil Nadu) which have per capita income above the national average,
- The conclusion emerges that the inter -state disparities have persisted in spite of the federal transfers. The fiscal disadvantaged States have lagged behind and are now termed BIMARU States instead of backward States.
- Independent rule with Nine Five Year Plans, Two Annual Plans, Two Rolling Plans, Eleven Finance Commissions' awards and transfer of financial resources from a number of Financial Institutions and Central Ministries has not brought much change in the relative position of States in terms of per capita income, which is at times taken as a sole determinant of economic development. The important question that immediately comes to mind is, as to what has the allocation of financial resources from the Union to the States achieved in regard to the reduction in inter-state socio-economic disparities? The disparity range in per capita income has increased from 0.31 in 1960-61 to 0.50 in 1970-71, 0.52 in 1980-81 and 1990-91 to 0.62 in 1996-97 as reflected in table 1.1 This clearly proves that economic disparities have more than doubled, if measured in terms of per capita income.

- The pattern of allocation of resources by different agencies has not been adequately progressive to mitigate the persisting inter-state disparities. Thus, the 'Directive Principles of State Policy' enshrined in our Constitution, which requires that the Government should strive to minimise inequalities amongst groups of people residing in different areas has not been adhered to.
- Disparity arises as a result of failure to exploit the hidden development potentials by the State governments, which the fiscal transfer mechanism in a federal structure must ensure by the transfer of resources in a manner that these fiscal disadvantages created by human, institutional and historical accidents are overcome by the States. The fiscal transfer must be in accordance with fiscal needs and fiscal capacities of the States.

The problem of inter-state economic inequalities in some form or the other exists in almost all federations. An economic or functional approach to equitable distribution of national funds among the States should be guided mainly by the consideration of each according to its needs. States do not have equal fiscal capacities, therefore, transfer of financial resources has to be, deliberately and consciously, far greater to backward fiscal disadvantaged States.

SECTION - 2 REASONS FOR PERSISTING AND WIDENING INTER-STATE DISPARITIES

Everyone perceives a backward State when he sees one. It is a State characterised by poverty, with beggars in the cities and villagers struggling out a bare subsistence in rural areas. It usually has insufficient roads, rail lines, inadequate supplies of power and light, poor communications, inadequate health services in terms of both hospitals and doctors, mass illiteracy, lack of institutions of higher learning. The poor and needy are at the mercy of village moneylenders, while the banking system caters to the rich and influential. In this landscape poverty of the masses, the State may have isolated islands of wealth with a few persons living in luxury. Without going into the mathematical technicality of economic variables and statistical tools the persisting inter-state disparities can be understood by a reader by answering a few simple questions —

Q. Why a man in a particular State is poor?

A. He has low income.

Q. Why he has low income?

A. The level of economic activity in that particular State is low.

Q. Why is that State persisting with low level of economic activity when the Nation is developing?

A. The income generating capacity of that particular State is low.

Q. Any reasons for low income generating capacity?

A. Two reasons. Nature did not bestow it with factor endowments for enhancing the rate of growth.

Man-made policies for enhancement of the potentialities are lacking and are not activated.

Inter-state disparities in India are an outcome of a combination of factors — histogeographic, socio-economic, political and above all State policies. Historically, inter-state disparities accentuated during the British rule. But we must ask our own swadeshi rulers as to what they have done in adhering to the 'Directive Principles of State Policy' enshrined in our Constitution, which requires that the Government should strive to minimise inequalities among groups of people residing in different areas. The important question that immediately comes to mind is, as to what has the allocation of financial resources by the multi-agencies of the Union government achieved in reducing inter-state disparities?

Geographically, certain areas remain inaccessible and hence, backward. The quality of land with which a State is endowed with effects its agricultural productivity. Mineral resources of the State determine the pace of industrialization. But mere presence of mineral resources is not sufficient to attract private investment. State must provide infrastructural facilities and enhance absorptive capacity. Bihar does not lack mineral resources, but it has remained at the last rank. It has failed to attract private enterprises due to poor techno-economic viability. Union Government did make sizeable public sector investments in backward States. Steel plants at Bhilai in Madhya Pradesh, Rourkela in Orissa and Bakaro in Bihar were set up. But these location decisions were in accordance with techno-economic viability also. These location decisions imaged a coincidence of twin objectives of reduction of inter-state disparities and techno-economic viability of a project. Yet, due to lack of ancillary industries and infrastructural facilities in these backward States, the assumed Spread Effects of these huge public investments did not emerge. Backwardness of these backward States persists till date.

Dr.(Mrs.) Hemlata Rao (1984) in her study has examined the factors responsible for inter-state disparities and to delineate homogenous regions in terms of both levels of development and topology of development, so as to have different groups of regions requiring different plan strategies at the micro-level.[1] On the theoretical side the study provides a method to measure development and disparity in quantitative terms. On practical side, it provides useful policy guidelines at the time of formulating policies for backward areas.

The study is specifically related to the State of Karnataka. It covers an analysis based on 19 districts and 175 talukas of the State for the period 1974-75 through 1979-80. The study is mainly based on the data collected from various departments of the Government of Karnataka. It has seven chapters in all. The first two chapters were on regional disparities and on measures and indicators of development respectively.

According to this study, there are three important underlying factors that lead to inter-regional disparities :

1. Historical factors. The regions which attracted the attention of various rulers and administrators, grew at a faster rate, and thus became developed regions. The development of metropolitan regions like Bombay, Calcutta, Madras and Delhi can largely be attributed to the historical factors.

2. Non-uniform distribution of natural resources. Prosperity of Punjab can largely be attributed to this factor.

Of course, human efforts along with natural endowments is a pre-requisite. Punjab State is held at an advantageous position with respect to both the factors.

3. Man-made factors. Some regions continue to remain backward due to the lack of human efforts, lack of entrepreneurship and lack of motivation. In addition, socio-economic factors, which are also man-made, are responsible for the inter-regional disparities. Once the unequal rates of growth developed, they would tend to perpetuate themselves due to the economies of concentration. Such regions exert centripetal forces and drain the marginal areas of any growth potential they might have had.

In the opinion of the author reduction of regional disparities requires a balance between goals of growth on the one hand and social justice on the other hand. Regions are to be encouraged to exploit their own development potentials and formulate development plans suitable to their needs, potentials and aspirations. Through federal fiscal transfers, Union government can equalize the resources in various regions.

In India, the policy framework evolved in this direction with a view to minimise and, if possible, eliminate regional disparities consisted in utilising the constitutionally provided statutory transfers through the Finance Commissions, non-statutory transfers through the Planning Commission and Central Ministries and Financial Institutions like, Commercial banks, Life Insurance Corporation and Industrial Finance Corporation. These multi-agencies can be made to channelise financial resources towards the backward regions.

S. Murty (1994) while evaluating the principles claimed to be kept in consideration by the Finance Commissions in the devolution of resources between the Union and the States, concludes that the scheme of distribution has not been able to lessen the inequalities between the States[2]. The author has brought out the growing inequalities as measured by per capita income levels of different States for the year 1950-51, 1960-61, 1970-71 and 1980-81. The emerging trend was widening of disparities over the years.

The range of disparities was Rs. 230.8 in 1950-51; Rs. 268 in 1960-61; Rs. 620 in 1970-71 and Rs. 1841 in 1980-81. Even the rates of growth of per capita income of different States had been very uneven. Punjab and Maharashtra achieved the highest rate of growth, with their income going up almost six times during this period. The rates of growth of per capita income in Rajasthan, Madhya Pradesh, Orissa, Manipur and Bihar have been low and have kept them in the clutches of poverty and at lower pedestal in the ranking of States according to per capita income, of course with an occasional change of the ranks here and there.

R.K. Sinha (1994) in the same book in his paper on "Fiscal Readjustment in India : Some Major Issues" has brought out the inter-state inequalities[3] :

"India is a Union of 22 States and 9 Centrally administered Union Territories. States differ from one another significantly in both physical and economic aspects. In terms of population the biggest State, Uttar Pradesh has 110 million people spread over an area of nearly 300 thousand square kilometers, giving a density ratio of 377. State of Kerala is 17th in area ranking, which has the highest density of population 654 people for one square kilometer". In terms of per capita income that the highest figure for Punjab (Rs. 2,027) was observed to be almost thrice as high than the lowest for Bihar (Rs. 737) for 1977-78, whereas the share of Bihar in the value of mineral production in the year 1978 was the highest (30 per cent) in the country.

In another paper entitled "Growing Discontent of States in Financial Relationship with the Centre : A case study[4]", Mr. Sinha while analysing the case of Bihar State concluded that all measures of inequalities, *i.e.*, the coefficient of variation, the range and the ratio between the highest and the lowest, confirm the existing disparities between States. The time period of study was 1949-50 to 1984-85.

The per capita income of Bihar was only 19 per cent below the national average in 1950-51 which declined to 40 per cent in 1984-85, the terminal year of the Sixth Five Year Plan. The per cent of population living below the poverty line was 49.5 as against the national average of 37.4. Index of infrastructural development of Bihar was 90 as against 100 of the country as a whole. Road length per lakh of population was only 119.73 kms, out of which only 40.16 kms were surfaced roads as against the national average of 219.75 kms and 96.86 kms respectively. Only 28.9 per cent of villages of Bihar were connected by all weather roads. The per capita consumption of electricity was only 91 kilowatt as against the national average of 154 kilowatt. Only 49.4 per cent of the villages of Bihar had been electrified upto March 1985 as against the national average of 64.0 per cent. According to the author such States like Bihar are a drag on the entire nation, because a developed India at the dawn of 21st Century cannot be imagined with poverty-stricken states like Bihar. Such poor States like Bihar should be in the list of special category States on the basis of their extreme poverty and should be provided lumpsum assistance, like other special category States to break the vicious circle of poverty and to fill the wide gap of regional imbalances.

Uma Datta Roy Choudhury (1992), analysed the relationship between the two indicators of development, *viz.*, per capita income and per capita household expenditure and ranks the States accordingly[5]. The States were ranked by the annual average rate of growth in 1960's, 1970's and 1980's, in descending order of the per capita income/consumption expenditure. The trend observed in the study indicated that the States which figure either at the top or at the bottom do so both for per capita State Domestic Product and per capita consumption expenditure. This was true of Punjab, Maharashtra and Gujarat with high levels of production and household consumption while Orissa, Bihar and Assam were at low levels. There were outstanding exceptions also — Rajasthan, Uttar Pradesh and Jammu and Kashmir, known to be comparatively underdeveloped States with low per capita income (below the all-India level in ranking except Jammu and Kashmir in 1985-86) but had high (above all India) level in per capita consumption — Rajasthan ranked second from the top only next to Punjab for all the years.

P.C. Sarkar (1994) assessed how far misdistribution of resources among the States had been corrected and whether there was a noticeable reduction in regional imbalances and changes in the ranking of the different States according to the degree of development[6].

The study was confined to fifteen major States which constituted 96 per cent of the total population (Assam was the fifteenth State to be included). It covered a span of twenty seven years, starting from 1960-61, the last year of the Second Five Year Plan and ending with 1986-87. In between these two extremes, data had been analysed for five bench-mark years, 1960-61, 1970-71, 1980-81, 1984-85 and 1986-87. Since this study was related to the Five Year Plans and imbalances, fourteen indicators related to those sectors where significant amount of Plan resources had been allocated or utilised in the States were considered. The sectors which are fully under Central government like railways, post and telegraph were not considered. An attempt was made to give adequate representation to sectors relating to power, irrigation and agriculture, industry, road and road transport and social services, since these sectors received on the average about 79 per cent of the public sector plan outlays in the first Seven Five Year Plans.

Besides, one indicator relating to overall development measure of the society such as "percentage of population below the poverty line" was also taken. A particular indicator within each of the sectors was selected on consideration of availability of data for the period of the study.

Most of the data was collected from Statistical Abstracts and Estimates of State Domestic Product of the Central Statistical Organisation (CSO), New Delhi as well as various publications of the Centre for Monitoring Indian Economy (CMIE), Bombay.

The analysis of ranking of States for all the five bench-mark years showed that Punjab and Haryana were the only agriculture based developed states throughout the study period and were able to occupy the first two positions in the development hierarchy. Bihar remained the least developed State and it had the maximum distance from Punjab.

Bihar and Uttar Pradesh maintained the least distance between them and, therefore, similarity was observed in their pattern of planned development from 1970-71 onwards. West Bengal which was in the third position in 1960-61 dropped to the ninth position in 1986-87. It had received half of the per capita cumulative plan outlay that was received by Punjab and Haryana while Bihar had got only one-third.

According to P.C. Sarkar, among the theories and models, developed to provide theoretical framework for understanding regional economic problems since the beginning of the mid-50s are : (1) export base models; (2) neo-classical model; (3) cumulative causation (Myrdal-Kaldor) model; (4) econometric models; (5) input-output models, and (6) multi-sectors development planning model (Richardson, 1973). But the applicability of these models is not universal. Their applicability would be determined in view of the differences in resource endowments, economic strategies, capital formation and institutions in the concerned country.

This study, in the Indian context, proved the hypothesis of an inverted U-shaped curve developed by Hirschman (1958), which was reinforced by the empirical statements from Kuznets (1957) and Williamson (1965), which stated that as an economy grows, regional disparities diverge at first only to converge later. The measures of inter-regional inequality trace out an inverted U-shaped curve overtime. There is a possibility of regional disparities changing with the stage of development. But at the same time, there is a need to reduce inter-regional disparities, which result in a conflict between the national objectives of efficiency and equality.

In India, not much work has so far been done from the theoretical point of view. B.S. Grewal's[7] study qualifies on this account and brings out the conflict between economic development and inter-governmental transfers.

Federal fiscal transfers are aimed to bring inter-State equality by the allocation of financial resources. But there is no general agreement as to what an equitable distribution means. Different individuals and schools of thought have different notions of distributive justice. All discussions agree to one common aspect which is termed as horizontal equity *i.e.,* equity between equals. Persons placed under similar circumstances should be treated in a non-discriminatory manner. The other aspect is termed as vertical equity — which is still a conflict-ridden issue. It refers to equality among unequals, which necessitates unequal treatment of unequals. Both are necessary, if federal fiscal transfer's objective of reduction in inter-state disparities is to be achieved. It is easy to observe them in a unitary form of government. But in a federal set-up even if both the Central and the State governments separately observe this principle in respect to their own fiscal operations, it will not guarantee that the equals living in different States would be treated equally by the total federal transfers. The net fiscal burden (taxes less benefits) on individuals is likely to be less in States having comparatively higher concentration of higher income population. The reason being that the higher income States can provide a comparable level of services at tax rates lower than in other States or a higher level of services at tax rates equivalent to those in other States. In both cases, the author holds "the fiscal residuum will be higher for the equally placed citizens living in higher income States. This amounts to fiscal discrimination on the basis of geographical location, and violates the principle of fiscal equity. This deviation from horizontal fiscal equity can be corrected if the Central government so adjusts the distribution of its own taxes and benefits that differentials caused by the activities of the State's fiscs are neutralised. This can be done through Central grants to lower income States. This neutralization is not confined to equal treatment of equals as between different States but is also extended to any attempt of a State government to treat the unequal's unequally in its own way". Equalisation, may mean equal fiscal burdens of the States, equal fiscal capacities of the States, or the equalisation of performance levels of the State services and so on.

Thus, equalisation may be a sound theoretical aspect of federal transfers and reduce inter-state disparities, but absolute equality of States in socio-economic field is not a feasible objective. Given the disparate factor endowments of different

States, complete equality of income will neither be a practicable nor a sensible objective. The author suggests that equity in the inter-state setting would be more meaningful if it is identified in terms of minimum level of social services and enables the State governments to attain and maintain these levels with reasonable tax burdens. This kind of floor-fixing may be applied to all socio-economic services.

Thus, the two objectives of allocative efficiency and equity taken separately give rise to a conflict. It is argued in various studies that one can be possible only at the cost of the other. Geographic transfer of tax revenues from richer States in order to provide amenities to people in resource-poor States will prevent the maximization of national product and strike at the very roots of allocative efficiency. But the federal fiscal transfers can be structured to bring a compromise between the two objectives. The pattern and arrangement of inter-governmental transfers should be one criteria which would reduce inter-state socio-economic disparities, which in the short run may not maximize national product.

SECTION - 3 METHODOLOGY APPLIED

Fourteen major States have been considered in the study. The hilly States of Assam, Jammu and Kashmir, Himachal Pradesh and the newly created States have not been included due to the non-availability of time-series data, their different dates of formation, their special problems and lack of comparative basis with other States. The States have been grouped into three categories :

Advanced States	:	Gujarat, Haryana, Maharashtra, Punjab, Tamil Nadu, West Bengal.
Middle level States	:	Andhra Pradesh, Karnataka, Kerala.
Backward States	:	Bihar, Madhya Pradesh, Orissa, Rajasthan and Uttar Pradesh.

This grouping of States as well as their serialisation (*i.e.*, serial numbering) are based on Sarkaria Commission Report (SCR). Thus, the serial number given to a State reflects its relative economic status in relation to the other States. The economic position of a State in this study is referred to as levels of development (SCR)[8].

Statistical tools used are : averages, coefficient of range, coefficient of variation, coefficient of rank correlation, average index and PQLI (Physical Quality of Life Index).[9] The first four terms are the specific defined terms but average index and PQLI have been used in a different context and they need to be explained. Average index term has been used when average of all fourteen States for a variable is equated to 100 and then relative figure for different States is calculated. Thus relative comparison of States is possible by the average level which has been taken as the bench mark or floor level or minimum required level for all socio-economic services.

Since the coefficient of range measures the disparity only at the two extreme ends, the coefficient of variation has also been calculated so as to study the variations based on all the observations. As the present study relates to the inter-state disparity, therefore, coefficient of range which depicts the gap between the two extreme States, has been more widely used then the coefficient of variation.

To measure the relative level of economic development, Physical Quality of Life Index given by Morris David Morris has been adopted and applied. The methodology of PQLI is the basis of building up a relative wealth indices of different States in order to bring out the disparities and fiscal needs of States which in other words are also the fiscal disadvantages or fiscal capabilities of States on a relative scale.

PQLI is based on a simple indexing system. For each indicator, the performance of individual state is placed on a scale varying from 0 to 100, where 0 represents an explicitly defined worst performance and 100 represents an explicit best performance. Once performance for each indicator is scaled to this common measure, a composite index can be calculated by averaging the indicators giving equal weight to each of them. The resulting PQLI thus is scaled automatically on an index of 0 to 100. There is, in fact a fixed range of worst to the best within which past, present and future performance can be incorporated. A scale with a fixed bottom and a fixed top implies that States can be expected gradually to close the gap between their current levels of performance and the explicitly defined and fixed upper limit. This is different from a measure like Gross National Product (in this study it implies Gross State Domestic Product). The Gross National Product as a statistical tool may not measure the inter-state economic disparities in an absolute and relative manner in a dynamic setting, as both the highest and the lowest income State would be increasing its income over the years and the gap will not show any definite trend of economic disparities. Thus it will fail to recognize improved performance overtime in a dynamic setting. In case of PQLI measure the worst State by improving its performance as the upper limit will always remain fixed at 100. Thus PQLI as a statistical tool is able to measure change in performance overtime. In a summarized form the PQLI will show how successful a State is in providing certain specific socio-economic services to its residents and how it performs overtime, the study of which is a must in a dynamic setting.

PQLI is to be applied to determine and formulate composite index of development/backwardness, which will identify the fiscal disadvantaged States and below average States in different indicators or development.

A composite index of development/backwardness will determine the existing inter-state economic disparities and thus indicate the fiscal needs of States by fixing a floor level or bench mark level of minimum needs which all States at least must provide. The optimum level of services achievable is the one existing in the most advanced State. But the most advanced State may not be the highest in all the indicators of economic development. Some States may be first in road km, the other may be best in health facilities and so on. Besides, in a dynamic setting even the most advanced State will still be growing and improving its socio-economic infrastructural framework.

Horizontal fiscal balance is a situation in which each State in a federal system has the capacity to provide services at a standard comparable to that of the other States, provided that it mobilizes its own resources at a comparable standard of its fiscal capacity.

However, State governments do not have equal fiscal capacity. Horizontal fiscal balance implies the existence of some form of revenue sharing arrangements or equalisation grants to remove the inequalities in fiscal capacity. Fiscal capacity has to be estimated by calculating the non-invested surplus of fourteen States. The formulae used for estimating absolute and relative fiscal capacity are as follows :

AFC = $NSDP_{FC}$ — (EC + G + PI)

RFC = AFC/$NSDP_{FC}$

AFC = Absolute Fiscal Capacity

RFC = Relative Fiscal capacity

NSDPFC = Net State Domestic Product at Factor Cost

EC = Essential Consumption

G = State Government Expenditure both on Revenue and Capital Account

PI = Private Investment

The methodology for estimating revenue capacity is based on the concept of essential consumption and essential investment. Essential consumption is based on the poverty line, which gives the minimum amount of purchasing power required to purchase the minimum consumption basket for subsistence plus something for incentives. The entire analysis is carried out at current prices. The price index and the poverty line used are State-specific. It is different for rural and urban population. Cost of living index of agricultural labour is used for rural population while for urban population cost of living index for industrial labour has been used. For the entire population of a State essential consumption is assumed to be uniform. The surplus that would emerge from the population whose actual consumption is less than essential consumption is not treated as a part of fiscal capacity available to a State for resource mobilization (it is not a part of non-invested surplus).

PI — private investment is assumed to be minimum at

15 per cent of Net State Domestic Product, so that minimum investment for development is ensured or at least not counted towards fiscal capacity of the States.

The required rate of investment is the product of three variables.

1. ICOR — Increment capital output ratio.
2. Rate of population growth.
3. Rate of growth of national income desired.

The whole analysis rests on the assumption that additional resource mobilization is not to be at the cost of investment or essential consumption.

To calculate fiscal capacity of States, gross and net economic surplus have been estimated. Gross economic surplus (GEC) is the difference between current output (income) of the State and current essential consumption, therefore :

GES = NSDP – EC

Net economic surplus is obtained by deducting private investment from GES. Therefore :

NES = GES – PI

This non-invested surplus is available to the States for mobilization of additional resources and is the estimated fiscal capacity of a State.

The analysis when extended to future projections on the basis of rate of growth of different variables is the estimated potential revenue capacity of the States, which can be utilized by the States in any manner they like — productive investments, unproductive investments or consumption on wasteful products (conspicuous consumption).

If mobilized for economic development of the State, it can generate services required in a State.

The estimates of fiscal capacity will yield the level of warranted own revenue to be raised by each State to help finance the level of warranted expenditure in the State. The amount of equalisation grant for each State may then be calculated simply as the difference between the warranted expenditure (need) and warranted revenue (capacity).

The role of the fiscal transfer streams has to be judged in this light. The criteria adopted by them have to be accepted or rejected according to the progressively achieved by them. Fiscal transfers have to aim at equalising the opportunities for growth to different States. The time period during which this has to be achieved must not be ignored. Since, each backward State represents a unique combination of factors and needs, no uniform policy or programme can be applied. The approach to remove inter-state disparities has to be location-specific and based on identification of the causes of backwardness as well as the potentials available for development. This is the very objective of this study.

Fiscal need is a relative concept which has to be considered always in relation to the availability of finances to different State governments. Low income States and low fiscal capacity States have to impose higher per capita taxes to maintain their public services at a level equal to advanced States. Therefore, the principle of fiscal need demands that they should be given higher per capita fiscal transfers from the Union. A fiscal transfer mechanism which gives all the States equal per capita shares is not really progressive. The aim of this study is to examine the role of these balancing devices in reducing inter-state economic disparities and providing at least minimum level of services to the citizens of India, no matter in which State they reside.

NOTES AND REFERENCES

1. Hemlata Rao : *Disparities and Development in India,* Ashish Publishing House, New Delhi, 1984.
2. Shandilya T.K. (ed.) : *Centre-State Financial Relations in India.* Deep and Deep Publications, New Delhi, 1994. Murty, S. : "An enquiry into the application of Finance Commission Principles", pp. 34-52.
3. *Ibid.* Sinha, R.K. : "Growing Discontent of States in Financial Relationship with the Centre : A case study". pp. 161-175.
4. *Ibid.*
5. Uma Datta Roy Choudhury : "Inter-State and Intra-State variations in Economic Development and Standard of living". *Economic and Political Weekly,* December 5-12, 1992. pp. 2651-2665.

6. Sarkar, P.C. : "Regional imbalances in Indian Economy Over Plan Periods", *Economic and Political Weekly*, March 12, 1994. pp. 621-633.
7. Grewal, B.S. : *Centre-State Financial Relations in India*; Punjabi University, Patiala, 1975.
8. Government of India : Report, New Delhi, December, 1987. This report is commonly known as *Sarkaria Commission Report (SCR)* and in the present study also it has been referred to as such.
9. Morris David Morris : *Measuring the Condition of World's Poor — The Physical Quality of Life Index*, Oversees Development Council, Perguman Press, New York, 1979.

2

COMPOSITE INDEX OF DEVELOPMENT AND FISCAL NEEDS OF THE STATES

The Seventh Finance Commission rightly observed that our focus should be specifically on how to place the financially weaker States in a position from where... they could get a better start than has been the case, in the past, in absolute terms as well as relative to the advanced States[1].

For reduction of inter-state disparities the States must be assured funds by the transfer of financial resources from the Union, so that they are able to provide services to their citizens at a comparable level, to other States. Certain basic socio-economic services ought to be provided to the citizens no matter in which State they reside. States having unequal fiscal capacity must be provided funds through the transfer mechanism to meet their fiscal needs, in a federal set up.

In relatively backward States, where the schools are being run without buildings, hospitals without adequate medicines or equipment, it is necessary to provide for these inadequacies. It is unrealistic to assume that these needs will be taken care of by the Planning Commission through the Central plan assistance. In backward States like Uttar Pradesh the major portion of the plan outlay is pre-empted by core sectors like irrigation and power. For improving the existing services and bringing them up to the desired level, necessary expenditure by the transfer of resources from the Union to the States must be provided.

The need for different public services may not be equally intense everywhere in a federation. Some State may be in need of irrigation facilities, whereas this may not be at all necessary in some other States because either there is adequate rainfall or private irrigation facilities are fully developed in that State. It may require some other public service.

Thus, equality in the inter-state setting may be more meaningful if it is defined in terms of minimum level of services required to be provided by the States to their residents with reasonable tax burdens. Floor fixing of the services is the essence of equality among States in the context of removal of inter-state disparities. The minimum per capita expenditure required for providing floor-level of services must be ensured to the States by fiscal transfer mechanism. This is a necessary condition for reducing inter-state disparities.

In this Chapter floor-fixing of required services is done and minimum per capita expenditure required to provide such services in States is estimated. In this context the chapter is divided into following four sections :

1. Preparing a relative composite index of development by selecting socio-economic indicators of development, which will reflect the existing level of services in different States. Section I is sub- divided into four sub-sections.

A. Selection of Indictors of Development :

B. Average Indexing of Physical Levels of Indicators (PQLI).

C. Absolute and Relative Performance of States by PQLI.

D. Performance of States on the basis of PQLI 1991 over PQLI 1971.

2. Fixation of minimum level of required services which all States must at least provide to their resident in a federal set-up. And also the optimum level of services which all States must strive for. The optimum level of services are the one existing in the best performance State (100).

3. Formulating a Need-based Table by computing the difference between the existing level of services (what is) and required level of services (what ought to be).

4. Per capita and total additional expenditure required to provide the needed services in which the States are below

the required level of services. That is, the per capita expenditure required to cover the gap between the existing and required level of services which must be ensured to the States through the transfer of resources from the Union, in the short run. Also, the additional expenditure required to achieve the optimum level of services in the long-run.

Thus, the reduction in inter-state disparities is considered in two time periods — in the short-run and in the long-run, providing for required level of services and desirable level of services respectively.

SECTION-1 COMPOSITE INDEX OF DEVELOPMENT

The first step requires the preparation of an index of development which will reflect the existing level of services in the States. For formulating such an index of development, the following procedure is adopted :

A. Selection of indicators. The choice of indicators for formulating the composite index of backwardness is very important. The choice is solely guided by the definition of economic development adopted. For this study economic development implies improvement in the material well-being of the people of a State which is measured by the eighteen indicators selected from various fields, *i.e.*, availability of infrastructural facilities, general amenities and public-utilities, agricultural inputs' availability and their consumption in a State and industrial sector's contribution to the States' material well being. Per capita income is widely accepted as a general measure of development. But income as an aggregative concept does not reflect structure of the State's economy. Different States may not be equally developed even if they have the same per capita income. At best, it can be taken as one of the indicators of development. No single indicator is comprehensive enough to measure the varying level of development *i.e.*, disparity among States. Thus, a composite index of a number of indicators is the best measure of disparity among States. The basic principle of these measures is to combine a number of economic, social and general factors in order to have an overall picture of the State and the material well being of its citizens.

Generally a number of indicators are interrelated and a few of them will best depict that field. For example, in case of health, hospital beds per lakh population and doctors per lakh population will be able to give some idea about the health facilities available in a State. Of course, the choice of indicators is subjective and suffers from this limitation.

A number of studies have been carried out to identify the backward States or regions of India. Ashok Mitra used some 35 indicators in an attempt to classify backward districts in India[2]. In Karnataka, the State Planning Department has been constructing a composite index of development at the district level for purposes of preparing Five-Year and annual plans[3]. They have selected some 22 indicators classified into six categories and assigned weights to them. They are :

(a) Demographic factors

(b) Occupational factors

(c) Land utilisation factors

(d) Agricultural development

(e) Industrial development

(f) Infrastructural development

The proper choice of indicators constitutes the crux of the methodology and this depends on the objective of the study and what is to be measured — disparity or only diversity, which are quite often used in the same sense. This study aims to study the inter-state disparities. Therefore, the choice of indicators does cover the above groups, but no weights have been assigned to the different indicators, as that would have introduced more subjectivity to the composite index. Three time-periods have been selected 1970-71, 1980-81 and 1990-91 over which the composite indices have been made (Table 2.1). In the present study eighteen indicators (Q) have been selected, *viz.*,

1. Per capita state domestic product
2. Per capita value added by manufacture
3. Percentage of urban to total population
4. Percentage of double cropped area

5. Area under HYV
6. Percentage of net irrigated area to net sown area
7. Percentage of working population to total population
8. Percentage of population above poverty line
9. Per capita electricity consumption (KWH)
10. Villages electrified as a percentage of total villages
11. Number of bank offices per lakh population
12. Hospital beds per lakh population
13. Doctors per lakh population
14. Number of post offices per lakh population
15. Percentage of literate to total population
16. Railway route per 000' square KM area
17. Road length per 000' square Km area
18. Number of registered vehicles per 000' persons

The indicators have been numbered from one to Eighteen. Therefore, for every state we have Q_1, Q_2, Q_3 — Q_{18} for three different years 1971, 1981 and 1991 representing three decades. This covers a period from 1970-71 to 1990-91 and evaluates the inter-state disparities during that period. The composite index of development is made in a dynamic setting. 1960-61 has been avoided due to non-availability of comparable data. Then Q_A and Q_C have been estimated :

$$Q_A \text{ — Average of 18 indicators} = \frac{Q_1 + Q_2 + Q_3 \cdots Q_{18}}{18}$$

There will be a Q_A for each State. Therefore, there will be 14 $Q_{A's}$ each for 1971, 1981 and 1991.

Since Q_A measures the level of development in an absolute sense, the performance of a State in relation to other States cannot be determined. Therefore Q_A has to be converted into Q_C by PQLI indexing of Q_{As} by applying the above given PQLI formula.

Q_C — PQLI of Q_A. By applying the PQLI formula to 14 Q_A. There will be a Q_C for each State. Therefore, there will be 14

Q_C. Each state will have Q_A 1971, Q_A 1981, QA 1991. By applying the PQLI to $Q_{A'S}$ we will have Q_C 1971, Q_C 1981 and Q_C 1991.

$$\frac{S-L}{H-L/100}, \text{ where}$$

S Stands for value of the concerned variable for which index is to be calculated of that particular indicator.

L The lowest value state for the indicator.

H The highest value state for that indicator. This will be equated to hundred. For example, supposing PQLI for Gujarat has to be calculated for Q1 1971 then the value are :

S = Rs. 827

L = Rs. 415 (of Bihar)

H = Rs. 1244 (of Punjab)

$$\text{Gujarat } Q_1 \text{ 1971} = \frac{827-415}{1244-415/100} = 50$$

(Values in the above example are from Appendix 2.1)

Thus, we get a composite index of development/ backwardness for the years 1971, 1981 and 1991. This table of composite index of development then is converted into a fiscal need table. This has been done only for the year 1991.

Conversion of Q table into N table : Example Q_1 indicator of all 14 States is averaged. For example, the average of Q_1 1991 is 41 (Table 2.3). This is fixed as the minimum or floor or bench mark level of service which each State must provide to its citizens. If a State has below average index it is depicted as N_1 for that State. Tamil Nadu has 34 Q_1 1991. Therefore N_1 is entered in N table for Tamil Nadu (Table 2.3). This is applied to all the indicators and a fiscal need table is formulated according to minimum average level of services to be, at least, provided by the States to the residents.

Thus, horizontal fiscal balance in this study is a situation in which each state in a federal system has the capacity to provide services at a standard comparable to that of the other

States, provided that it mobilizes its own resources at a comparable standard of its fiscal capacity.

18 indicators have been selected and coded as Q_1, Q_2...... Q_{18}. The existing physical level of services of the States are given in Appendix 2.1, 2.2 and 2.3 relating to three years, *i.e.*, 1971, 1981 and 1991 respectively. The choice of indicators is guided by the definition of economic development adopted in this study — the material well being of the people of a State.

B. To reduce the physical values to a single statistical unit-PQLI indexing is applied to the physical values. Table 2.1 is formulated on PQLI indexing basis. The formula has already been discussed in Chapter-1. The basic principle of this Table is to combine a number of social, economic and other related factors in order to have an overall picture of the State and the material well-being of its residents. For each indicator, the performance of individual State is placed on a scale varying from 0 to 100, where 0 represents an explicitly defined worst performance and 100 represents an explicit best performance. There is, in fact a fixed range of worst to the best performance within which past, present and future performance can be incorporated. A scale with a fixed bottom and a fixed top implies that the States can be expected gradually to close the gap between their current levels of performance and explicitly defined and fixed upper limit.

For instance, for Q_1 (per capita State Domestic Product) in 1971 the best performance State is Punjab (100). The worst performance State is Bihar (0). All the other States are at varying levels of per capita State Domestic Product. The maximum, these States could be expected to have in 1971 was the per capita State Domestic Product of Punjab. Similarly, the existing level of per capita State Domestic Product for 1981 and 1991 is given and measured on the PQLI scale. An index for each State in 1971, 1981 and 1991 is arrived at for each indicator. Each State has 18 Q_s for three different years, reflecting the existing level of services of the 18 indicators. In this manner physical values in different statistical units for 18 indicators are converted into a single unit Q. This will also

Table 2.1 (A)
Average indexing of Physical Level of Indicator (PQLI) in 1971

	Gujarat	Haryana	Maharashtra	Punjab	Tamil Nadu	West Bengal	Andhra Pradesh	Karnataka	Kerala	Bihar	Madhya Pradesh	Orissa	Rajasthan	Uttar Pradesh
Q_1	50	66	51	100	31	44	25	30	30	00	19	19	24	23
Q_2	59	32	100	19	36	51	03	26	12	05	02	02	01	00
Q_3	89	49	100	76	93	83	50	73	40	09	36	00	36	30
Q_4	09	84	19	100	31	66	16	00	53	56	09	72	16	72
Q_5	49	70	19	100	82	21	46	28	27	30	13	00	05	46
Q_6	09	56	00	100	55	28	30	09	19	33	01	17	09	50
Q_7	36	00	72	17	67	10	100	59	19	33	73	34	34	32
Q_8	53	80	35	100	27	27	47	35	37	18	16	00	63	31
Q_9	81	44	99	100	73	62	05	49	24	14	04	42	00	09
Q_{10}	19	89	38	48	90	27	28	33	100	04	04	00	04	14
Q_{11}	73	33	57	57	73	20	27	100	57	00	13	03	30	13
Q_{12}	14	38	72	45	38	79	55	83	100	00	00	12	34	07
Q_{13}	18	NA	42	100	42	58	13	19	19	09	00	10	01	02
Q_{14}	39	NA	19	100	45	16	64	35	29	19	00	29	22	19
Q_{15}	41	19	20	36	49	34	15	32	100	02	07	17	00	07
Q_{16}	50	67	16	100	56	93	17	09	36	59	03	00	14	58
Q_{17}	02	05	05	15	19	15	04	12	100	17	0.5	07	00	0.8
Q_{18}	97	19	100	39	40	56	34	65	58	00	13	05	43	03

Source : Computed from Appendix 2.1.
Note : NA stands for not available.

Table 2.1 (B)
Average indexing of Physical Level of Indicator (PQLI) in 1981

Q	Gujarat	Haryana	Maharashtra	Punjab	Tamil Nadu	West Bengal	Andhra Pradesh	Karnataka	Kerala	Bihar	Madhya Pradesh	Orissa	Rajasthan	Uttar Pradesh
1	57	74	66	100	25	29	30	29	20	00	11	14	19	13
2	62	57	100	37	46	39	09	21	19	10	14	00	04	10
3	84	44	100	69	92	64	50	74	30	03	37	00	39	27
4	07	81	12	100	24	54	12	00	12	49	08	65	11	65
5	44	68	32	100	59	33	45	04	54	56	06	07	00	50
6	18	67	00	100	43	33	31	08	04	33	06	20	13	60
7	14	11	75	17	79	11	100	63	00	19	73	38	24	16
8	67	90	25	100	17	17	30	35	62	00	02	15	35	12
9	76	73	89	100	51	18	15	39	15	00	12	22	08	02
10	100	100	100	100	100	08	94	89	100	08	42	00	21	18
11	48	45	33	100	42	07	25	65	90	00	12	10	18	05
12	84	08	46	38	22	?	11	22	100	00	0.4	02	10	03
13	27	NA	44	100	44	40	27	33	29	14	00	17	02	10
14	99	23	23	46	69	00	100	69	23	00	31	92	77	08
15	11	26	50	37	50	37	18	30	100	04	09	21	00	06
16	88	71	15	100	57	97	97	10	36	60	0.8	00	12	58
17	04	05	13	29	36	17	11	15	100	10	01	22	00	12
18	87	35	51	100	24	09	15	40	49	04	17	00	18	04

Source : Computed from Appendix 2.2.
Note : NA stands for not available.

Table 2.1 (C)

Average indexing of Physical Level of Indicator (PQLI) in 1991

Q	Gujarat	Haryana	Mahara-shtra	Punjab	Tamil Nadu	West Bengal	Andhra Pradesh	Karn-ataka	Kerala	Bihar	Madhya Pradesh	Orissa	Raja-sthan	Uttar Pradesh
1	55	84	85	100	34	37	36	34	24	00	24	16	24	16
2	63	45	100	80	58	07	06	22	23	04	09	09	00	04
3	62	39	88	61	100	55	70	84	55	00	55	56	38	24
4	00	82	16	100	73	77	12	03	35	37	16	62	10	54
5	16	19	53	40	23	27	35	24	00	27	51	20	20	100
6	19	77	00	100	39	31	35	11	04	40	13	24	16	62
7	66	0.7	86	00	88	09	100	79	03	09	85	47	57	09
8	87	87	43	100	33	46	36	36	74	13	00	20	56	33
9	70	76	58	100	46	13	38	37	24	00	31	21	32	18
10	100	100	100	100	100	14	100	100	100	11	56	00	29	19
11	54	42	32	100	44	12	28	78	84	00	20	22	26	10
12	44	08	45	37	23	24	11	22	100	00	01	32	10	08
13	36	NA	46	100	65	44	33	82	40	14	00	18	15	07
14	56	19	19	37	75	00	81	56	19	00	44	100	94	06
15	43	32	47	36	48	37	13	33	100	00	09	19	0.5	06
16	47	70	16	97	60	100	18	11	45	59	02	00	13	58
17	06	13	16	27	36	15	10	15	100	10	01	35	00	14
18	68	43	43	100	31	03	21	35	18	00	21	02	16	05

Source : Computed from Appendix 2.2.

Note : NA stands for not available.

help in measuring the absolute and relative performance of States overtime.

C. To measure the absolute and relative performance of the States : Absolute performance is measured by Q_A and relative performance by Q_C. Table 2.2 reflects the absolute and relative performance of the States over time.

Col.(2) is computed from the Q_s of 1971, 1981, and 1991. It is the average (Q_A) of the 18 Q's. For instance, in case of Gujarat 44 is the average of Q_1, Q_2....Q_{18} for 1971. Likewise the values of $Q_{A's}$ are computed for all the three years. This, composite index (Q_A) reflects the average development of a State for a particular year, or the average level of services existing in that State for that particular year. This gives an absolute level of the inter-state disparities in the concerned year. Comparison between 1971 and 1991 will reflect the performance of the States over two decades in absolute level.

Table 2.2

Absolute and Relative Composite Index of Development (1971, 1981 and 1991)

States	Average index of development (Q_A)			Composite index of development (Q_C)		
1	2			3		
	1971	1981	1991	1971	1981	1991
1. Gujarat	45	49	50	58	56	62
2. Haryana	45	51	49	58	59	61
3. Maharashtra	48	48	49	63	54	61
4. Punjab	69	76	73	100	100	100
5. Tamil Nadu	53	48	54	72	54	69
6. West Bengal	40	30	30	49	25	29
7. Andhra Pradesh	30	35	38	32	34	43
8. Karnataka	35	36	42	40	34	49
9. Kerala	48	49	47	63	56	57
10. Bihar	17	15	12	09	00	00
11. Madhya Pradesh	12	16	24	00	02	20
12. Orrisa	15	19	26	05	06	23
13. Rajasthan	19	18	26	12	05	23
14. Uttar Pradesh	23	21	26	19	10	23

Source : Col. (2) computed from table 2.1 and Col. (3) derived from Col. (2) by PQLI indexing.

The States having improved in absolute performance ($1991Q_A$ > $1971Q_A$).	: Gujarat, Haryana, Maharashtra, Punjab, Tamil Nadu, Andhra Pradesh, Karnataka, Madhya Pradesh, Orissa, Rajasthan, Uttar Pradesh.
The States having declined in absolute performance ($1991Q_A$ < $1971Q_A$).	: West Bengal, Kerala and Bihar.

The States which have declined in performance, over the years are West Bengal, an advanced State, Kerala a middle level State and Bihar a backward State.

But when PQLI indexing is applied to the $Q_{A's}$ and States grouped on their relative performance, then the above grouping of States changes.

D. States grouped on PQLI basis : Grouping of States is done on PQLI indexing. Col.(3) relates to PQLI indexing of Col.(2). For instance, for 1971 Punjab has the highest Q_A - 69, so, it gets 100 as the Q_C index of the best performance State. Madhya Pradesh has the lowest Q_A - 12, therefore, it gets 0 as the Q_C index for 1971. The PQLI indexing of the States is done for all the three years. Again, the States are grouped on the basis of performance in 1991 as compared to 1971.

The States having improved in relative performance ($1991Q_C > 1971Q_C$)	: Gujarat, Punjab, Andhra Pradesh, Karnataka, Madhya Pradesh, Orissa, Rajasthan, Uttar Pradesh
The States having declined in relative performance ($1991Q_C < 1971Q_C$)	: Maharashtra, Tamil Nadu, West Bengal, Kerala, Bihar
The State having the same performance ($1991Q_C = 1971Q_C$)	: Haryana.

The relative performance of Haryana has remained the same, though in an absolute level it indicated an improved performance. Maharashtra and Tamil Nadu, the two advanced States have also declined in relative performance over the years. Punjab has remained the best performance State. Bihar was the worst performance State for 1981 and 1991. Madhya Pradesh was the worst performance State in 1971.

The backward States, *viz.*, Madhya Pradesh, Orissa, Rajasthan and Uttar Pradesh indicated an improved performance on both the levels — absolute as well as relative.

SECTION-2 FIXATION OF MINIMUM REQUIRED LEVEL OF SERVICES

After, preparing a composite index of development reflecting the relative existing level of services in different

States in 1971, 1981 and 1991, the second step involved is the fixation of minimum required level of services which all States must at least provide to their residents. A decision has to be made regarding the level at which we want to equalise Q_C of different States, a necessary though not a sufficient condition for reduction in inter-state disparities.

Even if levels of social services are equalised at a minimum level, this does not ensure that inter-state economic disparities are minimized[4]. Approximate equality in the levels of social services is no doubt a necessary condition for narrowing down economic disparities, but it is by no means a sufficient condition. Economic disparities have their origin in differences in productive structure of State economies. A transformation of the economic structure of the backward States is required.

There are three possibilities of the level at which Q_C of different States can be equalised. The first possibility lies in taking a normative approach as adopted by the Ninth and Tenth Finance Commission as (dicussed in Chapter Four). This is arbitrary and subjective.

The second possibility is the level attained by the State having the highest PQLI (100) for that concerned indicator. For instance, Q_{12} — hospital beds per lakh population 292 are the highest in Kerala in 1991 (Table 2.3). Therefore, we fix 292 beds per lakh population as the required level of service for all the States. But, in a developing country like India, this may not be possible in the short run as financial resources may not be adequately available. The State having the lowest Q_{12} in 1991 is Bihar (40 hospital beds per lakh population). To close the gap and come at par with the level of Kerala, huge amount of resources are required, which may not be available immediately or in the short-run.

This should be kept as an optimum level of services desirable in the long run. Thus the level of services required to be achieved will depend upon the time period under consideration *i.e.*, short-run or long-run.

The third possibility is the average level of each indicator taken to be the minimum required level of service in the short-run, and the level of service of the best performance

State (100) taken to be the desirable level of service in the long-run. In the long-run, the States would be improving their performance and some other State may have the best performance, but the desirable level of services on PQLI indexing will remain fixed at 100.

In this study, 1991 is selected as the reference year for measuring the required level of services and conversion of Q-table into N-table (Need Table). The conversion is computed in Col.(2) relating to the Q_R *i.e.*, the required average level of service. For example, if we take Q_{12} (hospital beds per lakh population) then average level of Q_{12} in the fourteen States is 26 and this is the required Q_R for all the States, in the short run. Any State having Q_{12} below 26 (Q_R) will be marked as N_{12} indicating that it is below the minimum required level of Q_R and needs to improve this service. Therefore, N_{12} is entered for Bihar by converting Q table into N table, reflecting the physical need of the State in 1991.

The greater the N's in a State's column, the lower its level of development and higher its physical need. The N table clearly reflects the physical needs of the States and also brings out the existing inter-state disparities. The advanced States have more blank spaces and the backward States have more N's entered in their squares.

SECTION-3 IDENTIFICATION OF BELOW AVERAGE STATES

The third step requires the identification of States having below average 1991 Q_C. The grouping of States based on Table 2.4 is as follows :

The States having above average Q_C ($1991Q_C > 44$)	: Gujarat, Haryana, Maharashtra, Punjab, Tamil Nadu, Karnataka, Kerala
The States having below average Q_C ($1991Q_C < 44$)	: West Bengal, Andhra Pradesh, Bihar, Madhya Pradesh, Orissa, Rajasthan and Uttar Pradesh.

All the backward states have $1991Q_C$ below the average. Even West Bengal and Andhra Pradesh have a below average $1991Q_C$. Thus, in 1991, seven States had below average level of services. The fiscal transfer mechanism from the Union to

Table 2.3

Conversion of Q Table into N Table (1991)

Aver-age Q=OR	Gujarat	Haryana	Mahara-shtra	Punjab	Tamil Nadu	West Bengal	Andhra Pradesh	Karn-ataka	Kerala	Bihar	Madhya Pradesh	Orissa	Raja-sthan	Uttar Pradesh
41					N_1	N_1	N_1	N_1	N_1	N_1	N_1	N_1	N_1	N_1
31						N_2	N_2	N_2	N_2	N_2	N_2	N_2	N_2	N_2
57		N_3				N_3			N_3	N_3	N_3	N_3	N_3	N_3
47	N_4		N_4				N_4	N_4	N_4	N_4	N_4	N_4	N_4	N_4
32	N_5	N_5			N_5	N_5		N_5	N_5	N_5		N_5	N_5	
33	N_6		N_6			N_6		N_6	N_6		N_6	N_6	N_6	
46		N_7		N_7		N_7			N_7	N_7				N_7
47			N_8		N_8	N_8	N_8	N_8		N_8	N_8	N_8		N_8
40						N_9	N_9	N_9	N_9	N_9	N_9	N_9	N_9	N_9
66						N_{10}				N_{10}	N_{10}	N_{10}	N_{10}	N_{10}
39			N_{11}			N_{11}				N_{11}	N_{11}	N_{11}	N_{11}	N_{11}
26		N_{12}			N_{12}	N_{12}	N_{12}	N_{12}		N_{12}	N_{12}		N_{12}	N_{12}
34	N_{13}	NA					N_{13}			N_{13}	N_{13}	N_{13}	N_{13}	N_{13}
43		N_{14}	N_{14}	N_{14}		N_{14}			N_{14}	N_{14}				N_{14}
30							N_{15}			N_{15}	N_{15}	N_{15}	N_{15}	N_{15}
42			N_{16}				N_{16}	N_{16}			N_{16}	N_{16}	N_{16}	
22	N_{17}	N_{17}	N_{17}			N_{17}	N_{17}	N_{17}		N_{17}	N_{17}		N_{17}	N_{17}
29						N_{18}	N_{18}		N_{18}	N_{18}	N_{18}	N_{18}	N_{18}	N_{18}

Source : Computed from Table 2.1(1991 Q).

Note : NA stands for not available.

the States in three decades has not been able to provide resources to attain at least minimum average level of services in seven out of fourteen States. Thus, 50 percent of the States are still below average even after four decades of Independence.

Col.(2) of table 2.4 indicates the unit distance of below average States. Andhra Pradesh is only one unit away, whereas Madhya Pradesh, Orissa and Uttar Pradesh have covered only half a distance to the required average level. Rajasthan is 17 units away and West Bengal has to cover 13 units to be at par with the required average level of services.

SECTION-4 ADDITIONAL EXPENDITURE REQUIRED REFLECTING NEEDS OF STATES

The fourth and the last step requires the estimation of per capita and total additional expenditure required by the

Table 2.4
Minimum and Optimum Additional Per Capita and Total Expenditure Required (1991)

State	1991 QC	Unit distance from average QC(44)	Per capita expenditure (1991) (Rs)	Per capita minimum additional required expenditure (Rs)	Population in 1991 (Crores)	Total minimum additional required expenditure (Rs. Crores)	Unit distance from QC(100)	Per capita optimum additional desirable expenditure (Rs.)	Total optimum additional desirable expenditure (Rs. Crores)
1	2	3	4	5	6	7	8	9	10
1. Gujarat	62		1325		4.1		38	646	2649
2. Haryana	61		1455		1.6		39	663	1061
3. Maharashtra	61		1370		7.9		39	663	5238
4. Punjab	100		1660		2.0		00	00	00
5. Tamil Nadu	69		1183		5.6		31	527	2951
6. West Bengal	31	13	884	325	6.8	2210	71	1207	8208
7. Andhra Pradesh	43	01	988	25	6.6	165	57	969	6396
8. Karnataka	49		1107		4.5		51	867	3901
9. Kerala	57		1163		2.9		43	731	2120
10. Bihar	00	44	720	1100	8.6	9460	100	1700	14620
11. Madhya Pradesh	20	24	897	600	6.6	3960	80	1360	8976
12. Orrisa	26	18	962	550	3.2	1760	77	1309	4189
13. Rajasthan	21	23	1075	425	4.4	1870	77	1309	5760
14. Uttar Pradesh	21	23	890	575	14.0	8050	77	1309	1833
Average	44		1119						
Total				3600	78.8	27475		13226	67901

Source : Col.(4) *Centre for monitoring Indian Economy : Basic Statistics : States,* Monthly Review of the Indian Economy. Published by Economic Intelligence Service, Bombay, September 1994. Col.(6) *Census of India, 1991.*

Note : Per capita expenditure in Col.(4) includes total revenue and total capital expenditure and per capita is obtained by 1991, population.

below average States to come at par with average level of services in the short-run. Also, the estimation of per capita and total additional expenditure required by the States to come at par with the best performance State in the long-run.

This requires the estimation of additional expenditure required to bring below average States to the average level. The unit distance measured in physical terms has to be converted into monetary terms by multiplying with the cost per unit.

The average per capita expenditure in 1991 given in table 2.4 Col.(3) *i.e.*, Rs. 1119 is taken as the average cost per unit. With this per capita expenditure the average Q_C attained is 44 Col.(2). Therefore, average cost per unit in the short-run is Rs. 1119/44 = Rs. 25.

The per capita additional expenditure required in the short-run to bring below average level States at par with the average level is estimated in col.(5) by multiplying the unit distance of a State by Rs. 25. The total minimum additional required expenditure is indicated in col.(7), obtained by the product of per capita minimum additional required expenditure with the population of the concerned State. Bihar requires Rs. 9460 crores to come upto the average level of composite index of development. Uttar Pradesh requires Rs. 8050 crores. Madhya Pradesh requires Rs. 3960 crores. West Bengal, Andhra Pradesh, Orissa and Rajasthan require Rs. 2210, Rs. 165, Rs. 1760 and Rs. 1870 crores, respectively. This is the 'inescapable expenditure' required to provide floor (minimum) level of services in the below average level States. If measured on a relative scale, this was the fiscal need of the States in 1991, in order to reduce inter-state disparities in the short run.

In the long-run, the desirable level of services is the level of services existing in the best performance State, which will always be 100. In col.(8) unit distance of Q_C of States from 100 is computed. Except the best performance State all other States, even the advanced States, will have unit distance from 100. For the worst performance State *i.e.*, Bihar, the unit distance will be 100.

In order to convert the unit distance in-monetary terms, the cost per unit is estimated. In the long run, the cost per unit will be obtained by the per capita expenditure of the best performance State *i.e.*, Punjab which is Rs. 1660 and the Q_C attained by this expenditure is 100 (best performance State has 100 as the Q_C). Therefore, the average cost per unit in the long run is Rs. 1660/100 = Rs. 17.

The per capita optimum expenditure required in the long-run to attain desirable level of services is computed in col.(9) and the total optimum expenditure in col.(10) by the similar process as adopted for the short-run computation. This is the required expenditure to be provided by the States, to offer desirable level of services to their citizens and reduce inter-state disparities in the long-run. This brings out the fiscal need of the States in the long-run.

Our immediate aim should be to equalise Q_C at the average level of services. With development, the backward States will come out of the vicious circle of low internal resources and low absorptive capacity and achieve optimum level of services and close the gap between the most advanced State and their level of development. In the process inter-state disparities will be reduced, if not eliminated.

So far, the Finance Commissions have been adopting a gap filling approach. Non-plan budgetary gaps on revenue account are treated as fiscal needs of the States. Finance Commissions after reassessing the revenue and expenditure forecasts submitted by the States for the ensuing period, make them comparable and work out deficits on the non-plan current account of the State government's budgets, after excluding the share from the divisible pool of Central taxes. The States which have deficits are given grants-in-aid under Article 275. Thus, the estimated non-plan current account budgetary gaps based on mere growth rates of revenue and expenditure are treated as the fiscal needs of the State governments. The Finance Commissions can not reduce the shares of those States which have non-plan revenue surpluses after receiving tax shares. This provides growing amounts of unconditional grants to relatively better off States, whereas relatively backward

States are left with only gap filling fixed amounts of grants-in-aid. Such transfer mechanism has failed to reduce inter-state disparities.

The concept of fiscal equity in a federation implies that the imbalance between fiscal need and fiscal resources available to a State is rectified. Fiscal capacities of the States being unequal, the fiscal pressures on the citizens, no matter in which State they reside, can be equated, only by transferring resources to the States according to their fiscal needs and fiscal capacities. Then, inter-state disparities will be reduced to the minimum workable level.

A deliberate transfer of proportionately more fiscal aid to backward States has to be provided for to make them come at par with the minimum required floor level of services. Of course West Bengal and Andhra Pradesh also fall in this category of State needing proportionately more fiscal aid. Such an attempt might yield low economic returns in the short-run, but it will deploy inadequate national resources where they are most urgently needed to reduce the inter-state disparities. Citizens of the backward States have a right to at least average level of social and economic services, if not, that of the most advanced State.

NOTES AND REFERENCES

1. Government of India : *Report of the Seventh Finance Commission*, 1978, p. 81.
2. Ashok Mitra : Levels of Regional Development in India, *Census of India 1961*, para IA(1) as quoted in Hemlata Rao : *Regional Disparities and Development in India*. Ashish Publishing House, New Delhi, 1984, p. 31.
3. Hemlata Rao : *op. cit.*
4. Grewal, B.S. : *Centre-State Financial Relations in India*, Punjabi University, Patiala, 1975, p. 192.

3

FISCAL CAPACITY OF THE STATES

An economic or functional approach to equitable distribution of national funds among the States should be guided mainly by the consideration of each according to its needs. States do not have equal fiscal capacities, therefore, transfer and financial resources has to be, deliberately and consciously, far greater to the backward fiscal disadvantaged States. Horizontal fiscal balance implies the existence of some form of revenue sharing arrangements or 'equalization grants' to remove the inequalities in fiscal capacity, provided that the States mobilize their own resources at a comparable standard of their fiscal capacity. In this context this Chapter is divided into three sections :

Section 1. Methodology for computing fiscal capacity of the States.

Section 2. Computation of fiscal capacity of the States.

Section 3. Tax efforts of the States.

SECTION 1 – METHODOLOGY FOR COMPUTING FISCAL CAPACITY OF THE STATES

Fiscal or taxable capacity is both absolute and relative. Absolute taxable capacity is the maximum that a State can collect by way of taxes without producing unpleasant effects. The maximum limit to absolute taxable capacity is the limit of squeezability, where the entire net state domestic product is taxed. But no state can tax the citizens to the extent of taking away their entire income. States must leave some minimum level of income as non-taxable, needed for survival by its residents, as social human-beings. This is the essential consumption and should not be taxed.

Some part of Net State Domestic Product is also required for essential investment, both by the government and the private sector. The surplus, that emerges after providing for essential consumption and investment is the non-invested surplus and is the absolute fiscal capacity available to a State for revenue mobilization. By deducting the taxes already collected, the balance if any, is the potential taxable capacity which can be mobilized through additional taxation.

But it is quite possible that some States end up with negative absolute taxable capacity. The current Net State Domestic Product may be less than required for essential consumption and investment. The transfer of resources from the Union must ensure that the citizens of negative absolute capacity states are provided for, at least, minimum average level of services, at relative tax burdens.

This necessitates the estimation of relative fiscal capacity of States. The relative fiscal capacity of the States is the percentage of absolute fiscal capacity to the Net State Domestic Product. Higher the percentage, higher is the relative capacity of the States. The transfer of financial resources from the Union, must be in accordance with the relative fiscal capacity of the States. The States having negative absolute taxable capacity are bound to be at lower ranks, when ranked on a relative scale. Thus, necessitating proportionately larger transfer of funds from the Union, if fiscal equity is to be achieved, and reduction in inter-state disparities is the objective.

The above concept of absolute and relative taxable capacity is based on the assumptions of :

1. Closed economy : Inter-State flows of trade and foreign trade of States is excluded.

2. Zero substitution effect : Additional taxation will have no adverse effect on private investment.

3. Essential consumption is equal for the entire population of the state (AC=EC). (Though actual consumption for some sections of the State may be less than essential consumption)

4. The non-tax receipts such as fees, fines and profits of public sector undertakings are ignored, thereby equating the fiscal capacity of the State to its taxable capacity.

The estimates of fiscal capacity will yield the level of warranted own revenue to be raised by each State to help finance the level of warranted expenditure in the State, by its own efforts. The amount of equalization grant for each State may then be calculated simply as the difference between the warranted expenditure (need) and warranted revenue capacity.

The formula applied for computing the absolute and relative taxable/fiscal capacity is as follows :

$$AFC = NSDP_{FC} - (EC + G + P_1)$$

$$RFC = AFC/NSDP_{FC}$$

Where

AFC = Absolute Fiscal Capacity

RFC = Relative Fiscal Capacity

$NSDP_{FC}$ = Net State Domestic Product at Factor Cost

EC = Essential Consumption

G = State Government Expenditure both on Revenue and Capital Account

P_1 = Private Investment

Essential Consumption (EC) is the income necessary for physical survival and maintenance of the efficiency to live as human beings in a society and work as productive factor of production. Some income is required for social needs, the non-satisfaction of which may impair the physical efficiency. Socially accepted minimum needs are both food and non-food. Poverty line in monetary terms is the best proxy variable for estimating the minimum required socially accepted 'consumption basket' of the citizens of a State.

State-specific poverty lines if adjusted for current prices would give the required purchasing power to meet the specific calorie intake standard with some allowances for the non-food consumption needs.[1] This is the essential consumption of the residents of a State, which must be exempted from taxation to avoid undesirable effects on production.

India has both public and private sectors, therefore, both public and private investment has to deducted from the Net State Domestic Product in order to arrive at the fiscal capacity of the State. Public investment *i.e.*, State governments budgetary expenditure is the expenditure incurred by the State government both on revenue and capital account. All expenditure on the wages and salaries to the administrative staff of different departments, expenditure incurred on the maintenance of the offices, etc., must be deducted from the Net State Domestic Product to arrive at the taxable capacity of the State.

The major heads of capital expenditure are :

(a) Development outlay on social and economic services.

(b) Non-developmental outlay repayment of loans to the centre and loans to the local bodies and other agencies for social, economic and non-developmental purposes.

In a dynamic world, every economy has to divert a part of society's currently available resources to increase the stock of capital goods, so as to make possible an expansion of consumable output in future.[2] This will enhance the potential non-invested surplus of the State and hence enlarge the potential taxable/fiscal capacity of the State. The net economic surplus of a State is a reflection on the resources available to build up potential fiscal capacity. Converted in per capita terms, the availability of resources becomes more meaningful in reflecting the persisting inter-state disparities.

Minimum required private investment (P_1) by a State is of two types :

(a) Demographic investment is needed to maintain the growing population of the State at the same per capita income. It is determined by the rate of growth of population.

(b) Economic investment is required for raising the per capita income level. This is determined by the rate of growth of population and the desired rate of increase in National Product and Per Capita Income. The rate of national income growth is a function of capital-output ratio. Capital-output ratio (ICOR) expresses the relationship between the amount of increase in output (income) resulting from a given increase in the stock of capital.

Thus, minimum required investment in an economy is :

ICOR × Rate of Growth of Population × Desired Rate of Increase in Income (national and per capita).

SECTION 2 – COMPUTATION OF FISCAL CAPACITY

Computation of Fiscal Capacity is done in four steps :

A. Computation of Essential Consumption.

B. Computation of Gross and Net Economic Surplus.

C. Computation of Private Investment.

D. Computation of Absolute and Relative Taxable Capacity.

A. Computation of Essential Consumption

State-specific poverty line adopted to purchase the consumption basket differs significantly across the States. The food habits will depend on local availability as well as on consumer preferences. There are bound to be inter-state differences in terms of population structure, climatic and topographical considerations and so on. These need to be reflected in calorie requirements. But to ensure comparability across States the same 'consumption basket' has to be assumed in the base year. The base year for consumption basket is 1973-74 estimated at 1960-61 state-specific price base. Population has been categorized on the basis of residence into rural and urban population. For population living in rural areas referred to as rural population, Consumer Price Index for Agricultural Labourers (CPIAL) has been applied.

For population living in urban areas referred to as urban population, Consumer Price Index for Industrial Workers (CPIIW) has been applied. Essential consumption has been computed (Table 3.1-3.4) for fourteen major States for the years 1970-1971; 1980-1981; 1990-1991 and 1996-97 reflecting, the minimum purchasing power required in monetary terms to buy the basic needs' consumption basket by the residents of the respective States representing the four decades.[3]

Table 3.1

Per Capita and Total Essential Consumption of Rural and Urban Population (1970-71)

States	Price index 1970-71 rural	PCAEC rural (Rs.)	Rural population (lakhs)	TAEC rural Rs. (crores)	Price index 1970-71 urban	PCAEC urban (Rs.)	Urban pop-ulation (lakhs)	TAEC urban Rs. (crores)	TAEC rural + urban 1970-71 Rs. (crores)
1	2	3	4	5	6	7	8	9	10
Gujarat	173	392	192	755	184	539	75	404	1159
Haryana	194	412	83	342	199	488	18	88	430
Maharashtra	192	411	347	1426	191	560	157	879	2305
Punjab	194	412	103	424	197	484	32	154	578
Tamil Nadu	174	382	287	1096	182	494	125	617	1713
West Bengal	206	485	333	1615	183	494	110	543	2158
Andhra Pradesh	171	350	351	1228	194	513	84	431	1659
Karnataka	188	376	222	835	194	506	71	359	1194
Kerala	214	463	179	829	199	543	35	190	1019
Bihar	206	426	507	2160	196	519	56	291	2451
Madhya Pradesh	198	377	349	1316	196	542	68	369	1685
Orissa	212	421	201	846	188	552	18	99	945
Rajasthan	173	362	212	767	187	507	45	225	992
Utar Pradesh	183	350	759	2656	197	496	124	615	3271

Source : Col (2) : *Centre for monitoring Indian Economy, Basic Statistics, States,* Monthly review of the Indian Economy, Economic Intelligence Services, Bombay, Sep. 1994, Table 13.2.

Cols (4) and (8) : *Census of India*, 1971.

Col (6) Labour Bureau's series of Consumer Price Index Number of Industrial Workers, Ministry of Labour.

Cols (3) and (9) : Computed from Appendix I. See Note I for explanation.

Col (10) : Summation of Col (5) and (9).

Table 3.2

Per Capita and Total Essential Consumption of Rural and Urban Population (1980-81)

States	Price in 1970-71 rural (Rs.)	PCAEC rural (Rs.)	Rural population (lakhs)	TAEC rural (Rs. crores)	Prices 1980-81 urban (Rs.)	PCAEC urban (Rs.)	Urban pop-ulation (lakhs)	TAEC urban (Rs. crores)	TAEC rural & urban population (Rs. crores)
1	2	3	4	5	6	7	8	9	10
Gujarat	356	809	235	1901	434	1271	106	1347	3248
Haryana	437	928	101	937	470	1153	28	323	1260
Maharashtra	405	867	408	3537	461	1352	220	2974	6511
Punjab	437	928	127	1179	456	1116	47	524	1703
Tamil Nadu	391	858	325	2788	453	1230	159	1956	4744
West Bengal	400	942	401	3777	395	1066	145	1546	5323
Andhra Pradesh	353	722	410	2960	459	1214	125	1517	4477
Karnataka	398	796	264	2101	468	1221	107	1306	3407
Kerala	379	820	207	1697	458	1236	48	593	2290
Bihar	428	885	612	5416	433	1147	87	998	6414
Madhya Pradesh	433	824	416	3428	646	1283	106	1360	4788
Orissa	441	816	233	1901	428	1257	31	390	2291
Rajasthan	425	889	271	2409	473	1282	72	923	3332
Utar Pradesh	457	874	910	7952	454	1143	199	2275	10228

Source : Col (2) and (6) : Same as of table 3. Col (2) and (6).
Col (4) and (8) : *Census of India*, 1981.
Col (10) : Computed by adding col (5) and (9).

Table 3.3

Per Capita and Total Essential Consumption of Rural and Urban Population (1990-91)

States	Price in 1970-71 rural (Rs.)	PCAEC rural (Rs.)	Rural population (lakhs)	TAEC rural (Rs. crores)	Prices 1980-81 urban (Rs.)	PCAEC urban (Rs.)	Urban pop-ulation (lakhs)	TAEC urban (Rs. crores)	TAEC rural & urban population (Rs. crores)
1	2	3	4	5	6	7	8	9	10
Gujarat	742	1686	271	2569	923	2705	142	3841	8410
Haryana	930	1975	124	2449	973	2387	40	955	3404
Maharashtra	801	1715	484	8300	972	2851	305	8695	16995
Punjab	930	1975	143	2824	960	2349	60	1409	4233
Tamil Nadu	784	1720	368	3600	943	2560	190	4864	11194
West Bengal	842	1983	494	9796	822	2218	187	4148	13944
Andhra Pradesh	657	1336	486	6493	888	2349	179	4205	10698
Karnataka	807	1614	311	5019	996	2598	139	3611	8630
Kerala	939	2032	214	4348	862	2352	77	1811	6159
Bihar	906	1873	750	14047	872	2310	113	2610	16657
Madhya Pradesh	862	1640	508	8331	996	2754	153	4214	12545
Orissa	830	1649	274	4518	758	2226	42	935	5553
Rajasthan	885	1851	339	6275	951	2577	101	2603	8878
Utar Pradesh	960	1836	1115	20471	960	2418	276	6674	27145

Source : Col (2) and (6) : Same as of table 3.1 Col (2) and (6).
Col (4) and (8) : *Census of India*, 1991.
Col (10) : Computed by adding col (5) and (9).

Table 3.4

Per Capita and Total Essential Consumption of Rural and Urban Population (1996-97)

States	Price in 1970-71 rural (Rs.)	PCAEC rural (Rs.)	Rural population (lakhs)	TAEC rural (Rs. crores)	Prices 1970-71 urban (Rs.)	PCAEC urban (Rs.)	Urban pop-ulation (lakhs)	TAEC urban (Rs. crores)	TAEC rural & urban population (Rs. crores)
1	2	3	4	5	6	7	8	9	10
Gujarat	1356	3081	291	8966	1670	4894	164	8026	16992
Haryana	1325	2814	137	3855	1742	4273	48	2051	5906
Maharashtra	1498	3207	514	16484	1795	5264	351	18477	34961
Punjab	1052	2234	155	3463	1547	3785	69	2616	6079
Tamil Nadu	1480	3247	383	12436	1764	4789	211	10105	22541
West Bengal	1415	3332	537	17893	1394	3761	209	7860	25753
Andhra Pradesh	1297	2637	514	13554	1654	4375	207	9056	22610
Karnataka	1551	3102	333	10330	1873	4885	160	7816	18146
Kerala	1843	3988	221	8813	1732	4726	89	4206	13019
Bihar	1555	3215	799	25688	1500	3974	131	5206	30894
Madhya Pradesh	1576	2998	556	16669	1725	4770	1858	8824	25493
Orissa	1537	3054	292	8918	1354	3976	52	2067	10985
Rajasthan	1605	3357	377	12656	1661	4501	120	5401	18057
Utar Pradesh	1742	3331	1234	41104	1621	4083	333	13596	54700

Source : Col (2) : *Reserve Bank of India Bulletin*, December' 1998.

Col (4) and (8) : *Population projections for India and states*, New Delhi, Ministry of Home Affairs, Government of India, 1996.

Col (6) : Computed from *Statistical abstract of India*, Central statistical organization, department of statistics and programme implementation, Government of India, New Delhi, 1998, pp. 339-345.

B. Computation of Gross and Net Economic Surplus

Economic surplus is the non-invested surplus available with the State governments to be utilised for enhancing potential fiscal capacity.After providing for the essential consumption for the population and revenue and capital expenditure of the government from the Net State Domestic Product the balance if any, is available, both to the public and private sector for investment. It is the Net economic surplus and in per capita terms it reflects the capacity of the State to enhance the State Domestic Product which is the only way to increase fiscal capacity. Essential consumption is estimated at State-specific poverty line, a bare minimum. Private investment is also fixed at minimum. The important trends that emerge from table 3.5 to table 3.8 are :

- In 1970-71 Bihar has negative Net economic surplus (Rs. 130 crores) even when Bihar's Net State Domestic Products. Rs. 2245 (crores) was higher than that of Punjab Rs. 1436 (crores). Punjab had the highest Net economic surplus, because the population was second lowest (135 lakhs) only. Whereas Bihar had 563 lakhs population, with Uttar Pradesh leading at 883 lakhs.Therefore, Punjab had only Rs. 578 crores as essential consumption and Bihar had Rs. 2451 crores. This reduced Bihar's per capita Net economic surplus to (-)Rs. 23 crores. Punjab retained the first rank in total as well as per capita terms in Net economic surplus till 1996-97.
- Bihar emerged with a positive Net Economic Surplus in 1996-97 and Orissa in 1990-91.
- Punjab increased its per capita income 18 times and per capita Net economic surplus 21 times from 1970-71 to 1996-97.
- In 1996-97 Punjab's Net economic surplus was 13 times that of Bihar.

Table 3.5

Absolute and Relative Taxable Capacity, Gross and Net Economic Surplus of the States (1970-71)

(Rs. Crores)

States	Net State Domestic Product at factor cost	Essential consumption	Gross economic surplus	Budgetary expenditure on revenue and capital account	Net economic surplus	Private investment 15% of Col. (2)	Absolute taxable capacity	Relative taxable capacity (Per cent)
1	2	3	4	5	6	7	8	9
Gujarat	2189	1159	1030	312	718	328	390	18
Haryana	869	430	439	140	299	130	169	19
Maharashtra	3876	2305	1571	626	945	581	364	09
Punjab	1436	578	858	189	669	215	545	32
Tamil Nadu	2371	1713	658	401	257	256	99	04
West Bengal	3168	2158	1010	409	601	475	126	04
Andhra Pradesh	2523	1659	864	428	436	378	58	02
Karnataka	1858	1194	664	335	329	279	50	03
Kerala	1255	1019	236	230	06	188	(-)182	(-)14
Bihar	2245	2451	206	336	(-)130	337	(-)467	(-)21
Madhya Pradesh	1991	1685	306	298	08	299	(-)291	(-)15
Orissa	1037	945	92	190	(-)98	155	(-)253	(-)24
Rajasthan	1654	992	662	351	311	248	63	04
Utar Pradesh	4257	3271	986	516	470	638	(-)168	(-)04

Source : Col (2) : *Indian Economics Statistics, Public Finance,* Ministry of Finance, 1991, p. 78, col (3) : From table 3.1 col (10).
Col (5) : *Reserve Bank of India Bulletin,* Sept. 1972.

Note : Computed on the basis of formula : ATC = $NSDP_{FC}$ – (EC+G+P); RTC = ATC/NSDP; GES = NSDP-EC; NES = GES-G.

Table 3.6

Absolute and Relative Taxable Capacity, Gross and Net Economic Surplus of the States (1980-81)

(Rs. Crores)

States	Net State Domestic Product at factor cost	Essential consumption	Gross economic surplus	Budgetary expenditure on revenue and capital account	Net economic surplus	Private investment 15% of Col. (2)	Absolute taxable capacity	Relative taxable capacity (Per cent)
1	2	3	4	5	6	7	8	9
Gujarat	6585	3248	3337	1442	1895	988	907	14
Haryana	3032	1260	1772	607	1165	455	710	23
Maharashtra	15113	6511	8602	2613	4989	2267	2722	18
Punjab	4449	1703	2746	816	1930	667	1263	28
Tamil Nadu	7218	4744	2474	1686	788	1883	(-)1095	(-)15
West Bengal	8720	4223	3397	1552	1845	1308	537	06
Andhra Pradesh	7324	4477	2847	1610	1237	1099	138	02
Karnataka	5616	3407	2209	1302	907	842	65	01
Kerala	3823	2290	1533	856	677	573	104	03
Bihar	6360	6414	(-)54	1790	(-)1844	954	(-)21798	(-)44
Madhya Pradesh	6887	4788	2099	1589	510	1033	(-)523	(-)08
Orissa	3225	2291	934	877	(-)186	484	(-)670	(-)21
Rajasthan	4126	3332	764	1120	(-)1875	619	(-)2494	(-)60
Uttar Pradesh	14012	10228	3784	2669	1115	2102	(-)987	(-)07

Source : Col (2) : *Centre for Monitoring Indian Economy, Basic Statistics : States, Monthly Review of the Indian Economy,* Economic Intelligence Services, Bombay, September, 1994, table 10.4.
Col (3) : From table 3. 2 col (10).

Table 3.7

Absolute and Relative Taxable Capacity, Gross and Net Economic Surplus of the States (1990-91)

(Rs. Crores)

States	Net State Domestic Product at factor cost	Essential consumption	Gross economic surplus	Budgetary expenditure on revenue and capital account	Net economic surplus	Private investment 15% of Col. (2)	Absolute taxable capacity	Relative taxable capacity (Per cent)
1	2	3	4	5	6	7	8	9
Gujarat	23810	8410	15400	5475	9925	3571	6354	27
Haryana	12263	3404	8859	2395	6464	1839	4625	38
Maharashtra	56856	16995	39861	10821	29040	8528	20512	36
Punjab	16830	4233	12597	3367	9230	2524	6706	40
Tamil Nadu	25916	11194	14722	6607	8115	2887	4228	16
West Bengal	31386	13944	17442	6020	11422	4708	6714	21
Andhra Pradesh	30168	10698	19740	6570	12900	4525	8375	28
Karnataka	20847	8630	12217	4981	4236	2127	4109	20
Kerala	12062	6159	5903	3385	2518	1809	709	06
Bihar	22736	16657	6079	6216	(-)137	3410	(-)354	(-)02
Madhya Pradesh	26349	12545	13804	5937	7867	3952	3915	15
Orissa	11228	5553	5675	3046	2629	1684	945	08
Rajasthan	17804	8878	8926	4130	4796	2671	2125	12
Uttar Pradesh	48962	27145	21817	12306	9511	7344	2167	04

Source : Col (2) : *Centre for Monitoring Indian Economy, Basic Statistics : States, Monthly Review of the Indian Economy,* Economic Intelligence Services, Bombay, September, 1994, table 7.8.

Col (3) : From table 3.3 col (10).

Table 3.8

Absolute and Relative Taxable Capacity, Gross and Net Economic Surplus of the States (1996-97)

(Rs. Crores)

States	Net State Domestic Product at factor cost	Essential consumption	Gross economic surplus	Budgetary expenditure on revenue and capital account	Net economic surplus	Private investment 15% of Col. (2)	Absolute taxable capacity	Relative taxable capacity (Per cent)
1	2	3	4	5	6	7	8	9
Gujarat	66883	16992	49891	12574	37317	10035	27282	41
Haryana	30363	5906	24457	7893	16564	4560	12004	39
Maharashtra	155388	34961	120427	25005	95422	23310	72112	46
Punjab	40586	6079	34507	7547	26960	6105	20855	51
Tamil Nadu	69042	22541	46501	15402	31099	10350	20749	30
West Bengal	71568	25753	45815	13032	32783	10740	22043	31
Andhra Pradesh	75410	22610	52800	16265	36535	11310	25225	33
Karnataka	51360	18146	32214	11777	21437	7710	13727	27
Kerala	32387	13019	19368	8287	11081	4860	6221	19
Bihar	41188	30894	10294	2232	8062	6180	1882	4
Madhya Pradesh	55872	25493	30379	14216	16163	8385	7798	14
Orissa	20636	10985	9651	6310	3341	3090	251	1
Rajasthan	44307	18057	26250	10964	15286	6645	8641	19
Utar Pradesh	102864	54700	48164	23017	25147	15435	9712	9

Source : Col (2) : *Statistical Abstract Punjab*, 1999.

Col (3) : From table 3.4 col (10).

Table 3.9
Per Capita Net Economic Surplus and Ranking of the States

States	1970-71		1980-81		1990-91		1996-97	
	Per capita Rs.	Rank	Per capita Rs.	Rank	Per capita Rs.	Rank	Per capita Rs.	Rank
1	2		3		4		6	
Gujarat	269	3	556	4	2403	4	8201	4
Haryana	296	2	903	2	3941	2	8953	3
Maharashtra	487	4	794	3	3681	3	11031	2
Punjab	415	1	1109	1	4547	1	12036	1
Tamil Nadu	62	9	163	9	1454	7	5235	5
West Bengal	136	5	338	5	1677	6	4394	7
Andhra Pradesh	100	8	231	8	1940	5	5067	6
Karnataka	112	7	244	7	941	10	4348	8
Kerala	3	11	265	6	865	11	3574	9
Bihar	-23	13	-264	13	-16	14	867	14
Madhya Pradesh	2	12	98	11	1190	8	2181	11
Orissa	-45	14	-70	12	632	13	976	13
Rajasthan	120	6	-547	14	959	9	3076	10
Uttar Pradesh	53	10	100	10	684	12	1605	12

Source : Computed from Appendix 1.1 col (3), (4), (5) and (7).

C. Computation of Private Investment

The minimum required private investment in an economy is :

ICOR × rate of growth of population × desired rate of increase in gross national income and per capita income.

The value of the above variables for the Indian economy have been estimated and applied to the States.[4]

ICOR = 3.7

Rate of growth of population = 2.2 per cent. Desired rate of increase in national income = 4 per cent per annum. Substituting, the values in the above formula, the required rate of investment is 32.56 per cent per annum.

On the basis of experience, it can be implied that 45 per cent per annum investment is to be made by the private sector, therefore, the required minimum private sector investment is 14.65 (15 per cent) of national income[5]. Therefore, 15 per cent of Net State Domestic Product has been excluded from Net State Domestic Product to arrive at the fiscal/taxable capacity of the States. This portion of the Net State Domestic Product is not available for taxation. With economic development both ICOR and growth rat of population are bound to decline and then the same 15 per cent level of investment can bring about a higher rate of growth of income.

The rate of increase in per capita income can be obtained by subtracting the rate of growth of population from the rate of growth of national income. In this case the increase in per capita income will be 1.8 per cent per annum for the economy as a whole. The increase in per capita income will ensure higher living standards and improvement in the economic well-being of the people so that they can afford more and better amenities of life. For most people in the backward States, and population below the poverty line, it means having access to more and better food, clothing, shelter, education and medical facilities.

D. Computation of Absolute and Relative Taxable Capacity

Tables 3.5-3.8 reflect the absolute and relative taxable capacity of the States for the years 1970-71, 1980-81, 1990-91 and 1996-97 respectively. The analysis of the tables group the States as such :

States having	1970-71	1980-81	1990-91	1996-97
Positive absolute taxable capacity	Gujarat, Haryana Maharashtra, Punjab, Tamil Nadu, West Bengal, Andhra Pradesh, Karnataka, Rajasthan	Gujarat, Haryana, Maharashtra, Punjab, West Bengal, Andhra Pradesh, Karnataka, Kerala	All states except Bihar	All States
States having negative absolute taxable capacity	Kerala, Bihar, Madhya Pradesh, Orissa and Uttar Pradesh	Tamil Nadu, Bihar, Madhya Pradesh, Orissa, Rajasthan and Uttar Pradesh	Bihar	None

In 1970-71 five States out of fourteen had negative absolute taxable capacity. But in the next decade we had two more States, Tamil Nadu and Rajasthan, also in this group. Though Kerala had developed positive taxable capacity. But the decade 1990-91 ended with only Bihar, having negative fiscal capacity. Thus, the conclusion was clear that Bihar had negative non-invested surplus. The position has improved somewhat by 1996-97 with even Bihar emerging with positive absolute taxable capacity and that also higher than that of Orissa. Bihar had Rs. 1882.0 crores, absolute taxable capacity, whereas Orissa had only Rs. 25.0 crores, which was much lower than that of 1990-91 (Rs. 945.0 crores).

The ranking of the States in accordance with their relative fiscal capacities computed in Table 3.10 brings out the fact that Punjab State had the first rank in all the years, and the last rank was of Orissa in 1970-71, of Rajasthan in 1980-81, of Bihar in 1990-91 and again of Orissa in 1996-97.

On the basis of table 3.10 States can be grouped by their performance in relative taxable capacity in 1996-97 as compared to 1970-71.

Table 3.10

Ranking of States in Accordance with their Relative Taxable Capacity

States	Ranks according to relative taxable capacity 1970-71	Ranks according to relative taxable capacity 1980-81	Ranks according to relative taxable capacity 1990-91	Ranks according to relative taxable capacity 1996-97
1	2	3	4	5
Gujarat	3	4	5	3
Haryana	2	2	2	4
Maharashtra	4	3	3	2
Punjab	1	1	1	1
Tamil Nadu	5	11	8	7
West Bengal	6	5	6	6
Andhra Pradesh	9	7	4	5
Karnataka	8	8	7	8
Kerala	11	6	12	9.5
Bihar	13	13	14	13
Madhya Pradesh	12	10	9	11
Orissa	14	12	11	14
Rajasthan	7	14	10	9.5
Uttar Pradesh	10	9	13	12

Source : Computed from col (9) of tables 3.5-3.8 for the respective years.

Coefficient of rank correction between per capita income and relative taxable capacity for the respective years are :

1970-71	(+) 0.4
1980-81	(+) 0.87
1990-91	(+) 0.95
1996-97	(+) 0.92

The States having improved performance in relative taxable capacity.	Maharashtra, Andhra Pradesh, Kerala, Madhya Pradesh.
The States having declined in relative taxable capacity.	Haryana, Tamil Nadu, Rajasthan, Uttar Pradesh.
The States having maintained relative taxable capacity.	Gujarat, Punjab, Karnataka, West Bengal, Bihar, Orissa.

For reduction in inter-state disparities, the transfer of financial resources from the Finance Commissions should have improved the performance of backward states. Relative taxable capacity is nothing else but percentage of absolute taxable capacity to the Net State Domestic Product. The general viewpoint is that with the economic development of an economy, the absolute taxable capacity would increase, thereby, enlarging the base of States' own resources and relative taxable capacity would also increase.

The coefficient of rank correlation between per capita income and relative taxable capacity of the respective years 1970-71, 1980-81, 1990-91 and 1996-97 is positive and has increased from mere +0.4 in 1970-71 (Table 3.10) to as high as 0.96 in 1990-1991 and +0.92 in 1996-97. This clearly brings out the direct relationship between relative taxable capacity and per capita income.

The conclusion is obvious that backward States have not been able to overcome their inherent fiscal disadvantages, in spite of the massive progressive financial resource transfers from the Finance Commission. Such a situation after four decades of transfer of resources by the Finance Commissions cannot be lauded. It needs immediate attention and restructuring.

SECTION 3 – TAX EFFORTS OF THE STATES

But before deciding on the pattern of restructuring of the States' finances the tax efforts of the States in accordance with their relative taxable capacity must be viewed. 'Equity with incentive' should form the basis of federal fiscal transfers. Inefficiency of States in raising resources must not be subsidized at any cost. States must fulfill their tax obligations according to their relative taxable capacity. Tables 3.11-3.14 bring out the tax efforts of the States in mopping up their taxable capacity in relation to other States.

The term capacity relative of the States is the average index of States per capita income estimated in col. (3). The term effort relative is the average index of the percentage of per capita tax of a State to its per capita income.

The grouping of the states on the basis of capacity relative and effort relative is as follows :

	1970-71	1980-81	1990-91	1996-97
States having effort relative greater then their capacity relative (Er>CR)	Maharashtra, Tamil Nadu, Andhra Pradesh, Karnataka, Kerala, Bihar, Rajasthan, Madhya Pradesh	Tamil Nadu, Andhra Pradesh, Karnataka, Kerala, Bihar, Madhya Pradesh	Tamil Nadu, Andhra Pradesh, Karnataka, Kerala, Bihar, Madhya Pradesh, Orissa, Rajasthan Uttar Pradesh	Tamil Nadu, Karnataka, Kerala, Bihar, Madhya Pradesh, Orissa, Rajasthan, Uttar Pradesh
States having effort relative lower than their capacity relative (ER<CR)	Gujarat, Haryana, Punjab, West Bengal, Orissa, Uttar Pradesh	Gujarat, Haryana, Maharashtra, Punjab, West Bengal, Orissa, Rajasthan, Uttar Pradesh	Gujarat, Haryana, Maharashtra, Punjab, West Bengal	Gujarat, Haryana, Maharashtra, Punjab, West Bengal, Andhra Pradesh

Except for Tamil Nadu and Maharashtra in 1970-71, no other advanced State had effort relative greater than their capacity relative. Tamil Nadu has maintained this status till 1996-97. But Maharashtra has been having effort relative lower than capacity effort since 1980-81. The other advanced States Punjab, Haryana, Gujarat and West Bengal have effort relative lower than their capacity relative since 1970-71, whereas, Bihar needing aid desperately has effort relative greater than its capacity relative since 1970-71. Rajasthan, Madhya Pradesh, Orissa and Uttar Pradesh have also, effort relative greater than their capacity relative since 1990-91. Backward States collecting own resources more than what is warranted by their capacity is highly appreciable. At the same time advanced States must be penalized for not collecting taxes according to what their capacity warrants.

Table 3.11

Capacity Relatives and Effort Relatives of the States (1970-71)

States	Per capita income (Rs.)	Per capita capacity relative	Per capita tax (Rs.)	Tax effort (Per cent)	Effort relative
1	2	3	4	5	6
Gujarat	827	115	55	6.6	103
Haryana	960	134	56	5.8	91
Maharashtra	838	117	67	8.0	125
Punjab	1244	173	77	6.2	97
Tamil Nadu	669	93	50	7.5	117
West Bengal	781	109	43	5.5	86
Andhra Pradesh	627	87	44	7.0	109
Karnataka	664	92	48	7.2	112
Kerala	662	92	46	6.9	108
Bihar	415	58	29	7.0	109
Madhya Pradesh	575	80	34	5.9	92
Orissa	575	80	29	5.0	78
Rajasthan	618	86	37	6.0	94
Uttar Pradesh	603	84	32	5.3	83
Average Index	718=100			6.4=100	

Source : Col (4) *Reserve Bank of India* Bulletin, Bombay, Sept. 1972.

Table 3.12

Capacity Relatives and Effort Relatives of the States (1980-81)

States	Per capita income (Rs.)	Per capita capacity relative	Per capita tax (Rs.)	Tax effort (Per cent)	Effort relative
1	2	3	4	5	6
Gujarat	2238	127	158	7	109
Haryana	2601	147	184	7	109
Maharashtra	2466	140	182	7.4	116
Punjab	3169	180	211	6.7	105
Tamil Nadu	1541	87	133	8.6	134
West Bengal	1645	93	97	5.9	92
Andhra Pradesh	1659	94	110	6.6	103
Karnataka	1644	93	130	7.9	123
Kerala	1445	82	133	9.2	144
Bihar	1007	57	40	4	62
Madhya Pradesh	1240	70	73	5.9	92
Orissa	1308	74	51	3.9	61
Rajasthan	1429	81	68	4.8	75
Uttar Pradesh	1296	73	59	4.6	72
Average Index	1763=100			6.4=100	

Table 3.13

Capacity Relatives and Effort Relatives of the States (1990-91)

States	Per capita income (Rs.)	Per capita capacity relative	Per capita tax (Rs.)	Tax effort (Per cent)	Effort relative
1	2	3	4	5	6
Gujarat	5850	117	471	8.0	100
Haryana	7516	150	522	6.9	86
Maharashtra	7598	152	549	7.8	87
Punjab	8423	168	551	6.5	81
Tamil Nadu	4619	92	479	10	125
West Bengal	4794	96	359	7.5	94
Andhra Pradesh	4731	94	420	8.9	111
Karnataka	4631	92	443	9.6	120
Kerala	4032	80	451	11	137
Bihar	2650	53	231	8.7	109
Madhya Pradesh	4021	80	318	7.9	99
Orissa	3596	72	272	7.6	95
Rajasthan	4035	81	294	7.3	91
Uttar Pradesh	3557	71	271	7.6	95
Average Index	5004=100			8.0=100	

Source : Col (4) Bagchi Amaresh and Tapas Sen Trends and Plan Financing in the States, table 2.15, p. 90.

Table 3.14

Capacity Relatives and Effort Relatives of the States (1996-97)

States	Per capita income (Rs.)	Per capita capacity relative	Per capita tax (Rs.)	Tax effort (Per cent)	Effort relative
1	2	3	4	5	6
Gujarat	14875	136	1332	9.6	120
Haryana	16392	150	1155	7.1	89
Maharashtra	17666	162	1353	7.8	97
Punjab	18008	165	1223	6.7	84
Tamil Nadu	11708	107	1343	11.5	144
West Bengal	9579	88	571	6.0	75
Andhra Pradesh	10308	94	676	6.8	85
Karnataka	10504	96	1169	11.4	142
Kerala	10309	94	1260	13.9	174
Bihar	4231	39	242	6.3	79
Madhya Pradesh	7571	69	553	7.4	92
Orissa	5893	54	390	6.1	76
Rajasthan	8974	82	628	7.4	92
Uttar Pradesh	6713	61	402	6.0	75
Average index	10909=100			8.0=100	

Source : Total Tax Revenue – *Reserve Bank of India Bulletin,* Feb' 1999 and population – col (4) + col (8) of table 3.4

Economic backwardness is a self-feeding process. A backward state in a backward country has a double disability. The economic backwardness of the country and that of the state interact and reinforce one another. A large proportion of population in these states live under conditions that are unsatisfactory as compared to those prevailing elsewhere in India, conditions which can be defined sub-human in absolute terms. Everyone living anywhere in India is entitled to equity in respect of development of facilities like roads, electrification, health and education by the very fact of being a citizen of this democracy. Their development is a matter of national commitment. The traditional 'trickle down' theory of development has failed to automatically solve the problem of backward states.

So far the Finance Commissions have given grants-in-aid to states on the basis of budgetary deficits. The states find indirect (and unintended) encouragement, that no matter how poor their resource mobilization efforts are and how high their level of expenditure, the non-plan revenue gap would be made good by the Finance Commission. Had Punjab made efforts at revenue collection, at least equal to what it fiscal capacity warranted, it would not be in its present financial plight. There is no reason why the highest per capita income state, since four decades should hold a begging bowl before the Union Government.

'Equity with incentive' should form the basis of restructuring federal fiscal transfers. Inefficiency of states in raising resources must not be subsidized at any cost. Wastage of scarce financial resources is a luxury which we can ill-afford. So far federal transfers, in spite of being progressive have not been able to make any dent on inter-state disparities, even though the backward states, by and large have not been found lacking in self-help.

A state may be poor or rich, backward or advanced, underdeveloped or developed, in absolute terms, but its backwardness is relative to other States' development. This inter-state disparities can be reduced only when federal transfers are in accordance with the relative fiscal capacity of states.

NOTES AND REFERENCES

1. GOI, Planning Commission, *Report On Estimation of Proportion and Number of Poor,* New Delhi, July 1993.
2. Nurkse, R. : *Problems of Capital Formation in Under-developed Countries,* Oxford University Press, 1973, Delhi.
3. Note 1 : Explanation of the computation of tables (3.1-3.4).
4. Appendix 3.2 : Incremental capital output ratio on an average is 3.70. Appendix 3.3 : Annual rate of population growth is 2.2 percentage, on an average from 1951-91. Appendix 3.4 : Percentage of private and public investment during the five year plans, reflects that private investment was about 45 per cent on an average.
5. This is 45 per cent of 32.56 per cent required rate of investment per annum.

NOTE 1

Steps involved in computation of tables 3.1-3.4 relating to essential consumption.

Step 1 : Appendix 3.I per capita, per month and annual essential consumption is estimated at state specific poverty line in 1973-74, separately for rural and urban population at 1960-61 base for prices.

Step 2 : Table 3.1 per capita and total essential consumption of rural, urban and aggregate essential consumption is estimated for 1970-71. Col (3) is estimate of per capita annual essential consumption in monetary terms of rural population at 1970-71 state-specific prices. For example for Gujarat :

$$\text{PCAEC} = \frac{562}{248} \times 173 = \text{Rs. } 392$$

$$\frac{\text{PCAEC (rural) 1973–74}}{\text{Price (rural) 1973–74}} \times \text{Prices (rural) 1970-71}$$

$$\text{Source : } \frac{\text{Appendix 3.1 col.(4)}}{\text{Appendix 3.1 col.(2)}} \times \text{Table 3.1 col.(2)}$$

Col. (5) is an estimate of total annual essential consumption of rural population of the state obtained by the product of col. (3) and col.(4).

Col. (7) and col. (9) relate to urban population of the state and its total annual essential consumption computed in a similar manner.

Col (10) is the total essential consumption of the state obtained by the summation of col. (5) and col. (9). Tables 3.2, 3.3 and 3.4 reflect the total essential consumption of the states for the years 1980-81 1990-91 and 1996-97 respectively.

Since for the entire population of a state actual consumption is assumed to be equal to essential consumption, therefore, the surplus that would emerge from the population whose actual consumption is less than essential consumption is not treated as a part of fiscal capacity available to a state for resource mobilization. (it is not a part of non-invested surplus).

4

TRANSFER OF FINANCIAL RESOURCES FROM THE FINANCE COMMISSIONS AND INTER-STATE DISPARITIES

The objective of growth with social justice, in a developing federation like India, has to be achieved in a dynamic framework. India is a country where large-scale inter-state imbalances exist, either due to non-availability of infrastructural facilities and differential factor endowments, or due to inherent concentration of development in some regions. These inter-state disparities have to be reduced to attain the objective of social justice and at the same time ensure economic growth. Federal transfers from the Finance Commissions are expected to play a major role in this regard. Statutory transfers are meant to narrow down the differences in per capita State Domestic Product and standard of social and economic services being provided to the residents of different States.

The framers of the Constitution visualizing the lack of harmony between the financial resources and responsibilities of the States and in order to reduce the imbalances of resources between States, had suggested the appointment of Finance Commissions. Finance Commissions were required to play the role of a wise man, and a judge between the conflicting claims of the States on the one hand, and the Union Government on the other thus bringing in vertical and horizontal equity in the transfer of financial resources from the Union to the States.

In a federation, inter-governmental financial transfers cannot be settled once for all. There are problems of tax-sharing and grants which require changes with the changes in national objectives. But one objective which has been there since the First Finance Commission is the removal of disparities in the inter-state socio-economic levels of development.

This has to be achieved, keeping in mind the tax-efforts of the different States and economy in expenditure achieved by them. India is a developing federation and wastage of financial resources is a luxury which it cannot afford. Therefore, it is of utmost importance that all States put in the maximum effort to raise and conserve scarce financial resources. If the financial transfer scheme is based solely on the equalisation of general need of the States and neglects the resource mobilisation efforts of the States, some of the backward States might enjoy the benefits of federal transfers without making any efforts of their own. Such States live like parasites on the other States which are exploiting their financial capacities to go in for self help. They must get incentives for doing so by the Finance Commission's allocations inter-se. At the same time States with a perpetual begging bowl must be discouraged. No Finance Commission should subsidise inefficiency.

This chapter is meant to evaluate the role of Finance Commissions in reducing inter-State disparities. In this context the chapter is divided into four sections :

I. Role of first Eight Finance Commissions covering a period from 1952-53 to 1988-89. This period is termed as gap filling approach.

II. Role of instruments of fiscal equalization (Taxes and Grants-in-aid) in reducing inter-state disparities.

III. Role of the Ninth and Tenth Finance Commission covering a period from 1989-90 to 1999-2000, termed as normative approach period.

IV. A Note on Eleventh Finance Commission.

SECTION I : THE ROLE OF FIRST EIGHT FINANCE COMMISSIONS – GAP FILLING APPROACH

The role of the Finance Commissions would depend solely on the terms of reference given to them. The main terms of reference given to them under Article 280 of the Constitution are to make recommendations on the following :

(a) The distribution of the net proceeds of shareable taxes between the Union and the States and allocation of the shares inter-se.

(b) Principles governing the awards of grants-in-aid out of the Consolidated Fund of India and the sums to be paid to the States which are in need of assistance under Article 275 of the Constitution.

(c) Any other matter referred to the Commission by the President in the interest of sound finance. Under this clause the Finance Commissions are asked to examine and make recommendations on a number of issues such as :

(i) The distribution of net proceeds from additional duties in lieu of sales tax on sugar, textiles and tobacco.

(ii) The grants to the States in lieu of the repealed tax on railway passenger fares. This was first levied in 1957. It was abolished and merged in the basic fares with effect from 1.4.1961.

(iii) The grants to be made available to the States on account of abolition of wealth tax on agricultural property.

(iv) The distribution of the net proceeds of estate duty on other than agricultural land. But estate duty on property other than agricultural land was repealed in 1985.

(v) Providing relief or suggesting corrective measures on the debt position or non-plan capital gaps.

(vi) Study the problem of unauthorised overdrafts of certain States with the Reserve Bank of India and steps to be taken to avoid such overdrafts.

(vii) Relief expenditure to be provided to the States affected by natural calamities and

(viii) The scope for raising revenue from taxes and duties mentioned in Article 269 of the Constitution, which were not being levied.

The terms of reference determined the scope of the Finance Commission. The Finance Commission's purview did not include the following :

(a) Tax revenues of the States. Additional resource mobilisation by the States was treated as resources available for the five year plans.

(b) Discretionary plan grants from the Central Ministries.

(c) Central loans to the States.

(d) Grants-in-aid under Article 282 (capital grants).

This restricted the scope of Finance Commissions and led to the overlapping of functions between the Finance Commissions and the Planning Commission. Bifurcation of the grants under Article 275 as revenue grants and those under Article 282 as capital grants, was not intended under the Constitution. Grants-in-aid, now are recommended by two separate authorities. Under Article 275 grants-in-aid are provided by Finance Commissions to fill the budgetary gaps of the States and are termed as non-plan grants. Under Article 282 grants-in-aid are for plan requirements of the States for their capital budgetary needs, which are outside he purview of Finance Commissions, thereby restricting their scope. Finance Commissions cannot take a complete estimate of the budgetary needs of the States.

This demarcation between non-plan revenue grants-in-aid and plan capital grants came from the Third Finance Commission onwards. The first two Finance Commissions included plan requirements of the States while recommending grants-in-aid under Article 275. In fact, the Second and Third Finance Commissions were specifically asked through the terms of reference to take into account the financial requirements of the States for Second and Third Five Year Plan's respectively, while recommending grants-in-aid. The Third Finance Commission recommended not only special grants for development of roads in some poorer States but also grants for meeting 75 per cent of the plan component on the revenue budgets of the States.

But, the Union Government rejected these recommendations on the ground that they were outside the purview of the Finance Commission. Fearing, this type of rejection the Fourth and Fifth Finance Commission confined themselves to revenue grants under Article 275 excluding the requirements for five year plans of the States.

But, Sixth Finance Commission was asked to estimate the non-plan capital requirements of the States and also consider the extent of plan assistance provided to the various States on the recommendations of the Planning Commission. Thus, the bifurcation policy of the Union Government is not even consistent. This has resulted in shift of the policy about the relative importance/role of Finance Commission and Planning Commission and also about the grants-in-aid under Article 275 and Article 282. This could not have been visualised by the framers of the Constitution. When the Constitution was framed, Planning Commission was nowhere in picture.

The terms of reference nowhere have implied the gap filling approach adopted by the Finance Commission. Briefly, the Finance Commission's approach consisted of reassessing the revenue receipts and revenue expenditures of the States and making them comparable and projecting States' own revenues and expenditures for the period of the award.

After adjusting the estimated shares of assigned and shared taxes of the States, the Finance Commission recommended grants-in-aid to the States showing deficit in their revenue budgets.

It is here, that Finance Commission adopted a gap filling approach. The intention implied in the Constitution that financial transfers should be so allocated as to give each State according to its need was interpreted in this way by the Finance Commission. If deficits persisted even after tax devolution, then grants-in-aid were to be awarded to cover their budgetary deficit. Thus budgetary deficit was treated as fiscal need of the concerned State.

Fiscal need is a relative concept and in ad federal set-up, where the national objective happens to be growth with equity, it cannot be quantified in terms of budgetary deficit. Unequal States, with respect to fiscal capacities cannot be equated merely by meeting their budgetary deficits. The fiscal disadvantages of these States are relative to the advanced States.

Fiscal disadvantages of the States have to be measured in terms of revenue capacities both taxable and non-taxable and expenditure needs so as to make their standards of social and economic services comparable with those of the advanced States. This was the implied intention in the Constitution — to give each State according to its need. Such an approach, instead of the gap filling approach adopted by the Finance Commissions, would bring in equity in the development levels of the States and thus reduce inter-state disparities.

The Finance Commissions have always claimed that their intention and methodology adopted has been to reduce inter-state disparities. First Finance Commission agreed that the Scheme of distribution should attempt to lessen the inequalities between States[1].

Second Finance Commission implied the importance in the reduction in inter-state disparities while criticising the weight given to the collection factor in the distribution of income tax revenue as inequitable[2].

The Third Finance Commission in its approach considered the relative financial weaknesses of the State and disparity in the levels of development[3].

Fourth Finance Commission distributed part of the excise revenue on the basis of the relative economic and social backwardness of the State[4].

Fifth Finance Commission advocated a more positive redistribution policy which should distinguish between more advanced and less developed States[5].

Sixth Finance Commission stressed the need for using the mechanism of fiscal transfer from the Central Government to the States as a means of redressing regional imbalances[6].

Seventh Finance Commission moved in this direction when the shares of the States in the divisible pool of Union excise were determined by giving equal weight to the population factor, the inverse of the per capita State Domestic Product and the percentage of the poor in each State.

The importance of reducing inter-state disparities was aptly and amply brought out by the Sixth Finance Commission by acknowledging that the resources belong to the nation and they should be applied at points where they are most needed[7].

This is further strengthened by Hanson, "In general terms, it may be said that the Planning Commission works to the matching principle while the Finance Commission is more concerned with equalisation"[8].

To analyse the role of Finance Commissions in the reduction in inter-state disparities, ranking of the per capita state wise transfers has been computed in table 4.1. Financial transfers are aggregated till 1988-89 (Appendix 4.2). The coefficient of rank correlation is estimated with respect to per capita income for 1970-71, 1980-81, 1990-91 and 1996-97. Since the impact of federal transfers would be visible only after a time lag therefore coefficient of rank correlation has also been computed for 1990-91 and 1996-97.

The important trends that emerge from the analysis of table 4.1 are :

- The coefficient of rank correlation between per capita aggregate transfers and per capita income is negative, implying thereby that he transfer of financial resources from the Second to Eighth Finance Commission have been progressive with respect to per capita income of the States. (Per capita income is often considered as a proxy variable for economic development). But the degree of progressiveness has remained static over the years. The coefficient of rank correlation with per capita income hovers around –(0.7). A static progressiveness, has been inadequate to effectuate any reduction in the persisting inters state disparities.

Table 4.1

Ranking of States on the Basis of Per Capita Aggregate Federal Transfers and Per Capita Income

States	Per capita aggregate transfers 1957-58 to 1988-89	Per capita income 1970-71	Per capita income 1980-81	Per capita income 1990-91	Per capita income 1996-97
1	2	3	4	5	6
Gujarat	11	4	4	4	4
Haryana	14	2	2	3	3
Maharashtra	12	3	3	2	2
Punjab	13	1	1	1	1
Tamil Nadu	8	6	8	8	5
West Bengal	2	5	6	5	9
Andhra Pradesh	5	9	5	6	8
Karnataka	10	7	7	7	6
Kerala	3	8	9	10	7
Bihar	4	14	14	14	14
Madhya Pradesh	6	12.5	13	11	11
Orissa	1	12.5	11	12	13
Rajasthan	9	10	10	9	10
Uttar Pradesh	7	11	12	13	12

Note : Coefficient of rank correlation of per capita aggregate Transfers with per capita income. 1970-71 (-) 0.7
1980-81 (-) 0.7
1990-91 (-) 0.68
1996-97 (-) 0.77

Orissa has the first rank in the aggregate transfer of financial resources from Second to Eighth Finance Commission, but its thirteenth rank in per capita income in 1960-61, only improved marginally by one rank in 1990-91. This clearly implies that the financial resources transferred to Orissa, though were the highest, yet were not able to improve its position. Thus, the degree of progressiveness by the Finance Commission in the allocation of resources inter-state is inadequate. Hence, inter-state disparities persist till date, inspite of the huge quantum of federal transfers from the Union Government to the State Governments, by Finance Commissions.

On the whole the financial transfers from the First to the Eighth Finance Commission, even being progressive were not able to bring equality even in per capita income of the States, which is taken to be a summary indicator of inter-State disparities. This clearly implies that the degree of progressiveness achieved by the Finance Commissions was not adequate. The criteria adopted by the Finance Commissions in the devolution of tax-shares and awards of grants-in-aid inter-State require more progressiveness, if they are to reduce inter-state disparities.

There are two major sources of tax devolution to the States :

(a) Through tax on income other than agricultural income, though levied and collected by the Centre but compulsorily shareable between the Union and the States under Article 270 (1) of the Constitution. The proceeds attributable to Union Territories and taxes payable in respect on Union emoluments as also any surcharge which may be levied for the purpose of the Union are kept out of the divisible pool by the provisions contained in the Articles 270(2),(3),(4) and Article 271 of the Constitution[9].

(b) Through Union excise duties, if the parliament by law so provides. The criteria determining the size of the divisible pool has not been specified by any of the Finance Commissions. The Sixth Finance Commission discussed the determination of this quantum in the following words :

> "We have to strike a balance between the plea of the States for a substantial increase in the divisible pool and the needs of the Centre. We have also to ensure equity in the aggregate transfer of resources as between 'surplus' and the 'deficit states'. An enlargement of the divisible pool will confer disproportionately larger benefits on the surplus States than on the deficit States"[10].

The main irritants which the States want to be removed in this quantum determination are :

(a) The exclusion of corporation income tax from the compulsorily shareable proceeds.

(b) Abolition of estate duty on non-agricultural property as assigned tax under Article 269.

(c) Central Government increases its revenue by increasing administered prices, whereas States' divisible pool can be enhanced by increasing excise duties which are shareable with the States.

(d) States' sales tax is more buoyant than excise duties in lieu of sales tax on sugar, textiles and tobacco, which has been abolished.

The percentage of divisible pool to be shared between the Union and the States is given in table 4.2. The share of States in income tax has increased from 55 per cent as recommended by the First Finance Commission to 85 per cent by the Eighth Finance Commission. Thus, the exclusion of surcharges has been compensated by increasing the divisible pool by 30 per cent over the years.

The share of States in basic excise duties has increased from 40 per cent to 45 per cent by the Eighth Finance Commission but all the other Finance Commissions kept it very low between 20 to 25 per cent, with the exception of Seventh Finance Commission which increased it to 40 per cent.

But, gradually the number of articles considered for the shareable Union excise duty has been increasing. The First Finance Commission fixed the share of the States at 40 per cent of the net proceeds of duty on tobacco, matches and vegetable products. The Second Finance Commission included five more articles, taking the number upto eight. The Third Finance Commission, increased the number of articles to 35 and the share of the States was fixed at 20 per cent. The Fourth Finance Commission recommended the inclusion of all commodities excepting the duty on the generation of electricity 100 per cent of which was recommended to be

Table 4.2

Percentage of Divisible Taxes to be shared between the Union and the States on the Recommendations of First to Eighth Finance Commissions

Divisible items	First Finance Commission 1952-53 through 1956-57	Second Finance Commission 1957-58 through 1960-61	Third Finance Commission 1961-62 through 1965-66	Fourth Finance Commission 1966-67 through 1968-69	Fifth Finance Commission 1969-70 through 1973-74	Sixth Finance Commission 1974-75 through 1978-79	Seventh Finance Commission 1980-81 through 1983-84	Eighth Finance Commission 1952-53 through 1956-57
1	2	3	4	5	6	7	8	9
Income tax	55	60	62 2/3	75	75	80	85	85
Union excise duty	40	25	20	20	20	20	40	45
Number of dutiable articles covered	3	8	36	All	All	All	All	All

Source : Government of India : Reports of the respective Finance Commissions.

Table 4.3

Percentage Weightage Assigned to Different Criteria in the Allocation of Divisible Taxes (Inter State) as Recommended by the First to Eighth Finance Commissions

Criterion	Contribution	Population	Per capita Income distance	Per capita Income inverse	Indicators of backwardness	poverty	Revenue equalisa-tion	Plan difict
1	2	3	4	5	6	7	8	9
Income Tax								
First Finance Commission	20	80						
Second Finance Commission	10	90						
Third Finance Commission	20	80						
Fourth Finance Commission	20	80						
Fifth Finance Commission	10	90						
Sixth Finance Commission	10	90						
Seventh Finance Commission	10	90						
Eighth Finance Commission	10	22.50	45	22.50				
Union Excise Duty								
First Finance Commission	100							
Second Finance Commission	90			10				
Third Finance Commission	100							
Fourth Finance Commission	80			20				
Fifth Finance Commission	80			20				
Sixth Finance Commission	75	25						
Seventh Finance Commission	25	25			25	25		
Eighth Finance Commission	22.22	44.44	22.22					11.11

Source : Same as of table 4.2.

given to the States. The Eighth Finance Commission raised the share of the States to 45 per cent, of proceeds of Union excise duty on all commodities other than regulatory duties and special excise duties. The Seventh Finance Commission recommended 40 per cent among all the States and remaining 5 per cent to only those states having deficits after taking into account their share from all taxes and duties including their share in the 40 per cent of the proceeds of excise duties. Whatever be the quantum, the important aspect from the point of view of reduction in inter-state disparities is the inter-state distribution of this quantum and how far it is able to provide financial resources to cover fiscal disadvantages of the States and bring them at par with the development States.

Table 3.3 presents the percentage weightage assigned to different criteria in the allocation of divisible taxes *viz.*, income tax and Union excise duties. An examination of the table reflects that Finance Commissions regarded population of a State as the best proxy variable for the average needs of the States. When the national objective is family planning, the weightage to population in the allocation of divisible pool seems misplaced. Further the size of population is neutral to economic development and reduction in inter-state disparities. A major portion of divisible pool allocated on this basis will not raise or equalise the levels of development of backward States.

The next in importance are the general and specific indicators of backwardness. Their importance started from Seventh Finance Commission. Seventh Finance Commission brought in the criterion of per capita income distance and Eighth Finance Commission introduced inverse of per capita income. Earlier, Fourth and Fifth Finance Commission had used a composite index of backwardness in the distribution of basic excise duties. It was estimated by assigning equal weights to some selected socio-economic variables. But this small weightage to the criterion of backwardness has not been sufficient to reduce inter-state disparities.

Contribution is another factor considered for the distribution the shareable proceeds of the income tax.

Contribution, cannot be an adequate criterion as substantial part of tax receipts accrue in respect of incomes originating beyond the boundaries of respective States. For instance, the mineral resources of Bihar are exploited by companies which are situated in Calcutta. Hence the place of residence does not have any direct relationship with the source of income. Thus, there exists no economic justification for assigning 10-20 per cent weightage to contribution factor. The States cannot claim it as a matter of right or compensation — that they should be reimbursed according to their respective contribution to the proceeds of income tax.

At best we can say that the three important criteria of devolution of shareable proceeds of income tax and Union excise duties were population, contribution and a combination of the few indicators of backwardness. Population is neutral, contribution is regressive in nature and backwardness does not have adequate weightage. The net outcome is inadequate degree of progressiveness in the transfer of financial resources to the States.

After tax devolution some States may still have deficits in their revenue budgets. These are termed as post-devolution gaps in the non-plan revenue accounts of the States. The Constitution makers had realised that sharing of income tax and Union excise duties might not be adequate to cover the needs of the States. Therefore, Article 275 provided for grants-in-aid to such States which Parliament may determine are in need of assistance. This clearly shows that estimate of the need-revenue gap of the States is essential for determining the grants-in-aid to the States.

The objective of grants-in-aid should be to reduce the disparity among States on revenue account. With the passage of time the States should be able to overcome these inherent fiscal disadvantages.

This situation, was visualised by the framers of the Constitution, therefore, grants-in-aid were given the role of balancing the need and resource position of the States. The outcome was a gap-filling approach of the first eight Finance Commissions.

Grants-in-aid were to have a supplementary role in equating the fiscal capacities of the States. This has been clearly brought out by Ramanand Thakur[11]:

"The grants-in-aid overcome state financial disequilibrium resulting from the Constitutional arrangement and also help in correcting inter-state disequilibrium which results from heterogeneity".

The Finance Commissions were required to determine two aspects of grants-in-aid under Article 275.

(a) States in need of assistance after tax devolutions.

(b) Quantum of aid for each such state.

This required the Finance Commissions to evolve criteria for awarding grants-in-aid to the States, after reducing their non-plan (revenue account) budgets to comparable levels. This reassessed budget of the deficit States was termed as normal budget. This budgetary gap was treated as the fiscal need of States and grants-in-aid were awarded accordingly.

The following States could not qualify for grants under the award of the different Finance Commissions, and it can be safely assumed that they had a surplus budget (on non-plan revenue account).

Bihar did not get any grant-in-aid from the Third, Fourth and Fifth Finance Commissions.

Madhya Pradesh did not get any grant-in-aid from the First, Fifth and Sixth Finance Commissions.

Uttar Pradesh was not awarded any grant-in-aid from the first Five Finance Commissions.

But these States did have deficit budgets under the periods of these Finance Commissions, except for Madhya Pradesh which had a surplus budget in the Sixth Finance Commission period. This clearly implies that budgetary deficits of even backward States did not qualify them for grants-in-aid awarded by the various Finance Commissions.

Maharashtra is the only State which did not qualify for grants-in-aid under the awards of all the Finance Commissions.

But Maharashtra had a 'Surplus' budget only during the Sixth Finance Commission period.

Punjab got grants-in-aid only from the Second Finance Commission whereas it also showed a deficit budget for all the periods, except for the Sixth Finance Commission period.

Orissa is the only State to have qualified for the award of grants-in-aid by all the Finance Commissions. This State happens to be the highest deficit State.

Thus, there is no direct relationship between the budgetary gap of the States and grants-in-aid awarded by the various Finance Commissions, meaning, thereby, that certain other factors were taken into consideration while allocating grants-in-aid to the States.

The factors which should have been considered are :

(a) Tax efforts of the States : How far a State is going in for self-help and exploiting its own taxable capacity should be considered while awarding grants-in-aid to the States. But measuring tax efforts of the States requires the calculation of States' taxable capacities. The Second Finance Commission held that it is difficult to determine clear cases of inadequate taxation and if a State raised additional revenue which it promised for the plan it will have done its part[12].

(b) Economy in expenditure : The principle of self-help extends to economy in expenditure also. The objective of Article 275 is not to help States in balancing their annual budgets. The First Finance Commission clearly brought out by stating that if the amount of grants-in-aid were to be merely in proportion to the financial plight of a State a direct premium would be placed on impecurious policies and a penalty imposed on financial prudence[13]. But, again no direct measure is available to estimate the economy in expenditure achieved by the States.

(c) Standard of social services : Economic backwardness is clearly reflected by the level of social services in a State. The first step in the reduction of inter-state disparities is to make the level of socio-economic services in all the States, at least equal to a minimum national level. This will also ensure some equity to the residents of backward States, who because of their residence are made to suffer for want of adequate socio-economic services. Such States qualify for assistance under Article 275 which is especially designed to cover the 'needs' of the States. This will reduce the inherent socio-economic disparities among States.

A number of questions arise while determining the minimum national level of socio-economic services to be made available to all the citizens of India, no matter where they reside. Then, the selection of services to be included for availability in all the States is to be made. The existing level of services has to be estimated first and the services requiring consideration have to be determined. The assistance required to cover fiscal disadvantages of the States will depend on the cost per unit of different services, which will not be the same in all the States. Backward States will have higher cost per unit due to lower productivity of factors of production and non-availability of adequate infrastructure.

(d) Special obligations : Grants-in-aid must consider national commitments like refugee movements, international boundaries and natural calamities which become the special obligations of a State and cause an undue strain on its budget.

Finance Commissions agreed with these basic factors to be considered, while awarding grants-in-aid to the States, but differed with regard to the emphasis to be placed which would depend on the terms of references given to the various Finance Commissions. The Second and Third Finance Commissions were specifically asked to consider the plan requirements for the Second and Third Five Year Plans, respectively, as well as give due consideration to the tax efforts of the States. In the case of Fourth Finance Commission, nothing specific was mentioned about the plan component. It was asked to take into account the following :

(a) The expenditure devolving on the States for debt servicing;

(b) A part of the proceeds of estate duty were to be kept in a fund and

(c) Economy with efficiency in the administrative expenditure of the States.

Fourth Finance Commission excluded plan grants and special purpose grants from its awards. Whereas the Third Finance Commission had considered 15 per cent of the revenue component of the plans, to be the minimum that must be ensured to the States by way of grants-in-aid. This would enable the States to cover their fiscal need. Third Finance Commission wanted to increase the scope of scheme of assistance by including discretionary grants and loans also. It was not in favor of the artificial distinction between the plan and non-plan grants. In addition to the unconditional grants under Article 275, the First and the Third Finance Commission gave conditional grants for the upgradation of standards in primary education and communications respectively. But conditional grants were not related to the fiscal capacity of the States. Gujarat got communication grant under the award of the Third Finance Commission. Uttar Pradesh did not get any. The Sixth and Seventh Finance Commissions made provision for upgradation of administrative and social services to national standards, while computing the revenue gaps these specific purposes grants were awarded by the Sixth Finance Commission to all the States, except Tamil Nadu and Himachal Pradesh. They were irrespective of per capita income levels, per capita expenditure levels, per capita revenue surplus and per capita revenue raising capacity of the States.

The important conclusion that immediately comes to mind is that both tax devolution and grants-in-aid are not according to the fiscal capacity of the States. Therefore, it is very important to examine their role as instruments of fiscal equalisation in reducing inter-state disparities.

SECTION II : ROLE OF INSTRUMENTS OF FISCAL EQUALISATION IN REDUCING INTER-STATE DISPARITIES

Both tax devolution and grants-in-aid are means of assistance to the States. Tax shares are given without considering the financial status of the States, whereas grants-in-aid are specifically meant to cover the budgetary deficits of the States, after tax devolution. Therefore, Finance Commissions scrutinized the budgets of only those States which had post-devolution deficits on their non-plan revenue account. The other States were left with large surpluses.

Table 4.4 presents the ranks of the States in per capita tax shares and per capita grants[14]. The per capita income adopted for this analysis is of 1960-61 and that of 1990-91 through 1992-93 to make the analysis comparable. The analysis of the table brings out the following important conclusions :

(a) The negative coefficients imply that as per capita income increased the aggregate per capita tax devolutions and aggregate per capita grants decreased. Except for per capita tax shares with per capita income 1960-61 (+0.14) which is not significant, the conclusion emerges that tax devolutions and awards of grants-in-aid by the Finance Commissions have been progressive. Further, these coefficients have remained more or less the same over a period of four decades. The clear implication is that the degree of progressivity has remained the same, with only a slight insignificant variation.

(b) The coefficient of rank correlation is higher for aggregate grants as compared to aggregate tax devolutions. Therefore, it can be safely assumed that grants-in-aid are more progressive than tax evolutions. Their role in reducing inter-state disparities is far more than that of tax devolutions.

(c) The average of all fourteen States' per capita aggregate tax shares is Rs. 420, based on which the States can be grouped as follows :

State receiving above average aggregate per capita tax shares	: Gujarat, Maharashtra, Tamil Nadu, West Bengal, Kerala, Bihar

Table 4.4

Average Index and Ranking of States on the basis of Per Capita Aggregate Tax Shares and Grants (1956-57 to 1984-85)

States	Per capita aggregate tax shares		Per capita aggregate grants		Average index of per capita aggregate tax shares	Average index of per capita aggregate grants
1	2		3		4	5
	Rs.	Rank	Rs.	Rank		
1. Gujarat	453	2	13	11	108	19
2. Haryana	383^{L}	13	6	12.5	91^{L}	9
3. Maharashtra	458^{H}	1	3^{L}	14	109^{H}	4
4. Punjab	399	14	6	12.5	95	9
5. Tamil Nadu	430	4	16	9	102	23
6. West Bengal	438	3	86	5	104	123
7. Andhra Pradesh	410	10	94	4	98	134
8. Karnataka	407	11	58	6	97	83
9. Kerala	426	5	185	2	101	264
10. Bihar	423	6	3	7	101	47
11. Madhya Pradesh	414	8.5	14	10	99	20
12. Orrisa	420	7	288^{H}	1	100	411
13. Rajasthan	403	12	150	3	96	214
14. Uttar Pradesh	414	8.5	32	8	99	46
Average index	420 =100		70=100			
Coefficient of range	0.09		0.99			
Coefficient of variation	5 Per cent		116 Per cent			

Source : For cols. (2) and (4) Appendix 4.3 col.(8).

Coefficient of rank correlation between per capita income (1960-61) and

Per capita tax shares + 0.14 (Not significant)

Per capita grants (-) 0.6** (Significant at 5% level)

Coefficient of rank correlation between per capita income 1990-91 and

Per capita tax shares (-) 0.06 (Not significant)

Per capita grants (-) 0.63** (Significant at 5% level)

States receiving below average per capita tax shares	: Haryana, Punjab, Andhra Pradesh, Karnataka, Madhya Pradesh, Rajasthan, Uttar Pradesh
State receiving average aggregate per capita tax share	: Orissa.

Haryana and Punjab, the two advanced States have received below average per capita tax shares. This has brought down the coefficient of range to a very low level 0.09, whereas in case of per capita grants-in-aid, it is as high as 0.99.

All the backward States, except Bihar, have also received below average per capita tax shares. Thus, backward States have not been able to get tax devolutions in accordance with their fiscal disadvantages.

The other advanced States have received above average per capita tax shares. The highest average index of per capita aggregate tax shares is of Maharashtra (109).

(d) The average of all the fourteen States' per capita aggregate grants-in-aid is Rs. 70. The average index is calculated in Col.(5) based on which States can be grouped into two :

The states receiving above average aggregate per capita grants-in-aid	: West Bengal, Andhra Pradesh, Kerala, Orissa and Rajasthan.

The states receiving below average aggregate per capita grants-in-aid :

(a) Advanced States	: Gujarat, Haryana, Maharashtra, Punjab, Tamil Nadu
(b) Middle level State	: Karnataka
(c) Backward States	: Bihar, Madhya Pradesh and Uttar Pradesh.

Orissa has the highest index of 411 which is four times the average index (Rs. 70 equated to 100). Even then it has remained a backward State. This clearly makes one to conclude that the degree of progressiveness in financial transfers from the Finance Commissions has been inadequate. The inter-state disparities and fiscal disadvantages of the States call for a higher degree of progressiveness. Rajasthan has 214 as the index which is twice the average index. But Rajasthan has thirteenth rank according to the levels of development. The transfers from the Finance Commissions even of such a large magnitude have not made any significant affect on its relative status.

The other three backward states viz., Bihar, Madhya Pradesh and Uttar Pradesh have got a step-motherly treatment from the Finance Commissions. Their indices are below 100 at 47,20,46 respectively. Orissa got nearly twenty times more financial resources than Madhya Pradesh and nine times more than Bihar and Uttar Pradesh. Even West Bengal and Andhra Pradesh got six times more financial resources than Madhya Pradesh. This is not the approach to be adopted to reduce inter-state economic disparities.

The inherent fiscal advantage and disadvantage of States have remained the same , and so have the inter-state disparities. Grants-in-aid have not been sufficient even to bridge the budgetary gaps and their value gets eroded before they reach the States. This simply happens, because taxes are expressed as percentages in the divisible pool, while grants-in-aid are expressed in absolute amounts. Inflation increases the size of the divisible pool and consequently the tax shares of the States also increase. Grants-in-aid on the other hand get reduced in value by the time they are available for utilisation. Finance Commissions have made no provision for the rise in prices, intentionally or unintentionally. Thus, a more equitable distribution of financial transfers from the Finance Commissions is called for and that was expected from the Ninth and Tenth Finance Commission — A NEW APPROACH.

SECTION III : ROLE OF THE NINTH FINANCE COMMISSION AND TENTH FINANCE COMMISSION

The terms of reference of the Ninth Finance Commission were significantly different from the earlier Commissions. The Commission was to look into the following, besides tax devolution and its inter-state determination :

(a) Special problems of the States, if any and special requirements of the Union Government such as defence, debt servicing and other committed expenditure or liabilities.

(b) Adopt a normative approach, while reassessing the revenue receipts and expenditures (on revenue account) of the State Governments.

(c) Provide incentives for better resource mobilisation and economy in expenditure.

(d) To generate surplus for capital investments, besides balancing the receipt and expenditure on revenue account of both the States and the Union Government. For the first time the Ninth Finance Commission was asked to give recommendation on the followings aspects :

(a) To check the capital assets and requirements of the States which were backward in the general administration;

(b) To look into the non-plan capital gaps of the States and review the debt position of the States and

(c) To adopt a normative approach, rather than the gap filling mechanism.

In keeping with the terms of reference, Ninth Finance Commission considered the following objectives as a part of their approach :

(a) Phasing out the revenue deficit of the Union government and the States in such a manner that deficit was reduced to zero or a relatively small figure by March 31, 1995.

(b) Vertical and horizontal equity in the distribution of fiscal resources was to be the prime concern.

(c) Promotion of fiscal discipline and efficiency in the utilization of financial resources.

Implementation of these objectives called for a normative assessment of the fiscal needs and fiscal capacities of the respective governments. Here, was the basic departure from the gap-filling approach of the earlier Commissions. Second departure was in the inclusion of the plan component in the revenue budget of the States.

Ninth Finance Commission had presented two reports. The first report was presented for the year 1989-90 and the second report covered the period from 1990 to 1995.

Normative approach was used in the second report. Certain norms were applied in reassessing the revenue budgets presented by the State governments. The norms were derived on the basis of averages, for both revenue and expenditure of the State governments. On revenue side the norm was what a particular State would be able to raise by way of tax revenue, if it exploited its tax base to an average extent. For non-tax revenue the actual receipts have been used for certain items like fees, user charges, dividends and interest to be received. For major part of revenue expenditures, the average behavior was taken as the norm. Expenditure needs were estimated at justifiable costs of providing an average standard of service for general services and in case of social and economic services, the existing level of services was taken as the norm. Cost disability of the States was considered in arriving at this norm.

The Ninth Finance Commission used the normative approach only to arrive at the base year figures of the non-plan revenue receipts and the expenditure levels. For the subsequent years it used historical growth rates and projected the base year revenue and expenditure on revenue account.

The Ninth Finance Commission had worked out a scheme for determining the plan deficit grant[15]. This is given in table 4.5. The complete analysis is given in Appendix 4.1. An alternative scheme is also suggested. The Ninth Finance Commission's scheme for financing the deficits of the States on plan revenue account, was based on the following assumptions :

(a) Rs. 40,000 crores as the minimum total plan revenue expenditure for the fourteen States for a period from 1990-91 to 1994-95.

The inter-state allocation is explained by G. Thimmaiah, "In order to determine the shares of different States, their per capita plan revenue expenditure are estimated to range from a minimum of Rs. 325 for the state with the highest per capita expenditure Gujarat), to a maximum of Rs. 425 for the

Table 4.5

Scheme for Financing Revenue Plan Deficits Recommended by the Ninth Finance Commission and an Alternative Scheme (1990-91 to 1994-1995)

(Rs.Crores)

State	Minimum additional plan revenue expenditure	Plan revenue grant (Gadgil basis)	Post devolution non-plan surplus or deficit	40 % of surplus states	Resources for revenue plan financing under NFC	Budgetary position under NFC (only deficit states)	50 % plan revenue deficit grant awarded	Resources for revenue plan financing under AS	Budgetary position under AS
1	2	3	4	5	6	7	8	9	10
1. Gujarat	1779	435	3958	1583	2018				
2. Haryana	844	218	2505	1002	1220				
3. Maharashtra	3556	753	11526	4610	5363				
4. Punjab	926	258	1400	576	834	-92	46	1658	732
5. Tamil Nadu	2454	648	4296	1718	2366	-88	44	4944	2490
6. West Bengal	3264	634	1582	633	1267	-1997	998.5	2216	-1018
7. Andhra Pradesh	3345	947	4289	1716	2663	-682	341	5236	1891
8. Karnataka	2206	476	4670	1868	2344				
9. Kerala	1312	486	2	1	487	-825	4125	488	-824
10. Bihar	5046	1267	2575	1030	2297	-2749	1374.5	3842	-1204
11. Madhya Pradesh	3529	942	1229	491	1433	-2096	1048	2170	-1359
12. Orrisa	1602	493	-528	-	493	-1109	554.5	493	-1109
13. Rajasthan	2473	552	-486	-	552	-1921	960.5	552	-1921
14. Uttar Pradesh	7664	1891	-349	-	1891	-5773	2886.5	1891	-5773
Total	40,000	10,000							

Source : Guhan, S. : "Flawed Devolution Scheme", *Economic and Political Weekly*, June 9, 1990, p. 1270.

state with lowest per capita expenditure (Bihar). The difference in per capita non-plan expenditure on social and economic services in 1994-95 between each state and the state with the highest per capita expenditure was first worked out. These differences were expressed as a ratio of the maximum difference obtained and then multiplied by hundred. The value obtained represent the additional amount of per capita expenditure required to supplement the minimum specified 325"[16]. The inter-state allocation is given in col.(2).

(b) Rs. 10,000 crores as the plan revenue grant to be allocated on the basis of Gadgil formula. For determining this amount total assistance under Gadgil formula in 1989-90 (Rs. 1450 crores) was taken as the base and it was expected to grow at 10 per cent per annum. On this assumption the States could be expected to get Rs. 10,000 crores of grant. Its inter-state allocation is given in col.(3).

(c) Only 40 per cent of the post-devolution surplus of the States was to be counted towards the resources available for financing their plan revenue expenditure. Col.(4) indicates the post-devolution non-plan surplus or deficit of the States and col.(5) is the estimated 40 per cent available for the plan finance.

The alternative scheme takes 100 per cent post-devolution surplus of the States, col.(4), as resources available for financing the plan revenue expenditure.

To make the analysis concise the Ninth Finance Commission Scheme is coded as 'NFC' and alternative scheme as 'AS'. The analysis of the two schemes divides the States into four groups :

1. States which were not the concern of the Ninth Finance Commission (Post-devolution surplus States) : Gujarat, Haryana, Maharashtra, Karnataka
2. States qualifying for plan deficit grant under 'NFC' but not under 'AS' : Punjab, Tamil Nadu, Andhra Pradesh
3. States qualifying for plan deficit grant under both the : West Bengal, Kerala, Bihar, Madhya Pradesh

schemes, but deficit reduced under 'AS' (Post-devolution surplus States)

4. States with post-devolution deficit qualifying for plan deficit grants under both the schemes. : Orissa, Rajasthan and Uttar Pradesh

Table 4.6 reflects the percentage weightage assigned to different criteria in the allocation of divisible taxes across the States as recommended by the First and Second report of the Ninth Finance Commission and also by the Tenth Finance commission. The main points of differences in the approaches of the Ninth Finance Commission in its two Reports and Tenth Finance Commission as follows :

I. In the inter-state allocation of income tax :

(a) Contribution as a criteria was discarded by the Tenth Finance Commission, whereas the two Reports of the Ninth Finance Commission gave 10 per cent weightage to it.

(b) Population had a reduced weightage (22 per cent) under the Tenth Finance Commission when compared with 22.50 per cent under the two Reports of the Ninth Finance Commission.

(c) The weightage given to per capita income distance criterion was increased to 60 per cent by the Tenth Finance Commission from 45 per cent recommended by the Ninth Finance Commission in both the Reports.

(d) Per capita income inverse criterion was discarded by the Tenth Finance Commission, whereas it had 11.25 per cent weightage assigned by the two Reports of the Ninth Finance Commission. Tenth Finance Commission considered per capita income distance criterion as more progressive than per capita income inverse, therefore weightage to the former was increased to 60 per cent while latter was discarded.

(e) Indicators of backwardness as a criterion was not adopted by the Ninth Finance Commission in its First Report, but was given 11.25 per cent weightage in the Second Report. Tenth Finance Commission also gave 10 per cent weightage

Table 4.6

Percentage Weightage Assigned to Different Criteria in the Allocation of Divisible Taxes (Inter-State) as Recommended by the Ninth and the Tenth Finance Commission

First Report of the Ninth Finance Commission (1989-90)

Criterion\ Tax	Contri-bution	Popula-tion	Per capita income distance	Per capita income inverse	Indica-tors of back-wardness	Poverty	Tax Effort	Post devolu-tion deficit
1	2	3	4	5	6	7	8	9
Income tax	10.00	22.50	45.00	11.25		11.25		
Union excise duty		22.22	44.44	11.22		11.11		11.11

Source : Government of India : First Report of the Ninth Finance Commission 1989.

Second Report of the Ninth Finance Commission (1990-91 through 1994-95)

Criterion\ Tax	Contri-bution	Popula-tion	Per capita income distance	Per capita income inverse	Indica-tors of back-wardness	Poverty	Tax Effort	Post devolu-tion deficit
1	2	3	4	5	6	7	8	9
Income tax	10.00	22.50	45.00	11.25	11.25			
Union excise duty		25.00	33.50	12.55	12.50			16.50

Source : Government of India : Second Report of the Ninth Finance Commission 1990.

Tenth Finance Commission (1995-96 through 1999-2000)

Criterion\ Tax	Contri-bution	Popula-tion	Per capita income distance	Per capita income inverse	Indica-tors of back-wardness	Poverty	Tax Effort	Post devolu-tion deficit
1	2	3	4	5	6	7	8	9
Income tax		20.00	60.00		10.00		10.00	
Union excise duty		16.84	50.53		8.42		8.42	15.79

Source : Government of India : Second Report of the Tenth Finance Commission 1995.

to it, and introduced to specific indicators of backwardness (area adjusted and index of infrastructure).

(f) While in the First Report of the Ninth Finance Commission poverty was assigned 11.25 per cent weightage, the Second Report as well as the Tenth Finance Commission discarded this criterion altogether.

(g) Tax effort was a new criterion introduced by the Tenth Finance Commission and it was given 10 per cent weightage.

II. The inter-state allocation of Union excise duty is as follows :

(a) The weightage given to population as a criterion was reduced by the Tenth Finance Commission to 16.84 per cent as compared with 22.22 per cent in the First Report and 25 per cent in the Second Report of the Ninth Finance Commission.

(b) The weightage given to per capita income distance criterion was increased to 50.53 per cent by the Tenth Finance Commission compared with 44.44 per cent in the First Report of the Ninth Finance Commission and 33.50 per cent in the Second Report of the Ninth Finance Commission.

(c) Per capita income inverse criterion was discarded by the Tenth Finance Commission, whereas it had 11.22 per cent and 12.55 per cent weightage respectively in the First and Second Report of the Ninth Finance Commission.

(d) Indicators of backwardness as a criterion was introduced by the Ninth Finance Commission in its Second Report and assigned 12.50 per cent weightage to it. This was reduced to 8.42 per cent by the Tenth Finance Commission.

(e) Poverty was assigned 11.11 per cent weightage by the First Report of the Ninth Finance Commission, but was discarded in its Second Report and was also discarded by the Tenth Finance Commission.

(f) Tax effort as a criterion was introduced by the Tenth Finance Commission was assigned 8.42 per cent weightage.

(g) Post devolution deficit was assigned 11.11 per cent weightage by the First Report and 16.50 per cent by the Second

Report of the Ninth Finance Commission. While the Tenth Finance Commission assigned 15.79 per cent weightage to it.

The Tenth Finance Commission submitted its Report on March 14, 1995. The terms of reference did not explicitly require the Commission to adopt a normative approach in reassessing the receipts and expenditures on the revenue account of the States and Union Government. The objectives placed before the Commission were :

1. Balancing receipts and expenditures on the revenue account.
2. Generating (revenue) surplus for capital investments.
3. Reducing fiscal deficit of the States.
4. Tax efforts of the States and potentials for raising additional taxes to be considered.
5. Maintenance expenditure on plan schemes to be completed by March 1995 and maintenance of capital assets to be taken into consideration.
6. The requirements of the States for modernisation of administration and for upgrading standards in the non-developmental sectors and services.
7. The need for ensuring reasonable returns on investment by States in irrigation and power projects.
8. The scope for better fiscal management consistent with efficiency and economy in expenditure.

To fulfill these objectives an integrated view of Central and State finances was required both of the plan and non-plan revenue and expenditure. But the Commission limited itself to non-plan revenue and expenditure.

Certain rates of growth over the period (1995-2000) were assumed by the Commission[17].

1. Gross Domestic Product at 5 per cent to 6 per cent per annum.
2. Annual inflation was assumed to decline gradually from 7.5 per cent to 5 per cent.
3. Norms for the growth of non-tax revenue receipts were fixed at,

(i) 4 per cent for outstanding loans.

(ii) For dividends between 1,4 and 6 per cent depending on the type of enterprise.

(iii) Power projects returns were fixed at 3,5 and 7 per cent over the years.

(iv) Returns from the state road transport undertakings were determined at 2.5 per cent rising to 6 per cent by the terminal year.

4. For non-plan revenue expenditure the trend growth rate was around 18 per cent which was very high and was unlikely to be met from revenue receipts. The rate of increase was fixed at 1.5 per cent per annum for sectors/services like education, interest payments, maintenance of capital assets and committed liabilities. A higher rate of growth (2.5 per cent per annum) was provided for health and family welfare and for elementary education for those states where literacy levels were below the national average.

The Commission was silent about the (projected) liabilities that may arise from the recommendations of the Fifth Pay Commission. This came into sharp focus when the recommendations of the Fifth Pay Commission were implemented and the States had to meet this financial liability.

The important change that the Commission made was in the States' share in the divisible pool. It was reduced by 7.5 per cent in income-tax (from 85 per cent in the previous three Finance Commissions to 77.5 per cent); and increased by 2.5 per cent in Union excise duties (from 45 per cent to 47.5 per cent).

The Tenth Finance Commission introduced a set of new indicators of backwardness, viz., area adjusted and index of infrastructure giving them 10 per cent weightage.

The area adjusted and index of infrastructure were introduced to account for the additional administrative and other costs that a State with a larger area has to incur in order to deliver a comparable standard of service to its citizens. This required adjustment due to the following factors. Beyond a point, the additional cost may not increase; Smaller States would have to incur certain minimum costs in governmental expenditure; States in hilly areas have higher administrative costs.

The Commission was of the view that "some corrections are required for the relative disparities in infrastructure as between the States"[18]. An aggregate index of infrastructure of social and economic services was made. The respective shares of the States were derived, on the basis of this index using the distance method.

Tax effort was given 10 per cent weightage. Tax effort index was obtained as the ratio of States' per capita own tax revenue to the square of its per capita income. The reasoning given for squaring per capita income in the denominator is to give incentive to poorer States if they exploit their tax-base as much as a richer State.

The criterion of inverse income was dropped and instead per capita income distance was given greater weightage to the extent of 60 per cent in income-tax and 50.53 per cent in Union excise duties, on the assumption that the degree of progressivity is more in distance criterion than in inverse criterion.

The Commission observed that the population criterion, by itself is not progressive as it imparts the same per capita share to States, irrespective of the level of per capita income. But the reduction in weight from 22.5 per cent to 20 per cent was only a marginal reduction. Since the influence of population as a scale factor is spread across all criteria; this reduction was considered to be of relatively insignificant importance by a Report of Reserve Bank of India[19].

But this indicates a significant change when compared with earlier Finance Commissions (First to Eighth) where population was given 80 to 90 per cent weightage. The weightage of population in income tax devolution and Union excise duties came down from to 22.50 and 25 respectively as recommended by the Ninth Finance Commission and was further reduced to 20 and 16.84 per cent by the Tenth Finance Commission.

For awarding grants-in-aid the Commission was specifically asked to consider upgradation of the standards in non-developmental sectors. After identifying the areas for upgradation, the Commission did not recommend upgradation grants for those States which were assessed to have an overall pre-devolution non-plan revenue surplus, viz., Gujarat, Haryana, Karnataka and Maharashtra.

Grants-in-aid for gap-filling under Article 275 were also recommended to Andhra Pradesh, Bihar, Orissa, Rajasthan and Uttar Pradesh on the basis of post-devolution deficit.

Table 4.7 indicates the ranks of the States on the basis of total per capita transfer, tax shares and grants-in-aid as recommended by the Tenth Finance Commission. An analysis of this Table brings out the following conclusions :

(a) The coefficients of rank correlation of per capita transfers, tax devolutions and grants-in-aid with per capita average income 1990-91 through 1992-93 are negative. Thus, the transfers of financial resources by the Tenth Finance Commission are progressive. The degree of coefficient of rank correlation is -0.86 for per capita transfers, -0.90 for tax shares and -0.37 for grants-in-aid.

(b) The degree of progressivity is nearly twice as much greater in tax shares than in grants-in-aid. The reduction in the weightage to population, seems to have increased the progressivity of tax devolutions. Thus, tax devolutions as an instrument of fiscal equalisation, which go a long way in reducing inter-state disparities, have achieved far more than grants-in-aid could. Grants-in-aid seem to have retained its nature as a fiscal residuum.

A comparison with the financial transfers (aggregate) from First to Eighth Finance Commission is very essential to judge the effect of change in criteria adopted by the Tenth Finance Commission. And a comparison of the coefficients of rank correlations in the financial transfers with per capita income is equally important. The examination of these coefficients of rank correlations brings out the following conclusions :

Table 4.7

Ranking of States on the Basis of Per Capita Tax Shares and Per Capita Grants and Total Transfers Recommended by the Tenth Finance Commission (1995-96 to 1990-2000)

(Rs.)

States	Per capita tax shares	Per capita grants	Per capita total transfers
1	2	3	4
1. Gujarat	11	5	11
2. Haryana	14	9	14
3. Maharastra	12	14	13
4. Punjab	13	4	12
5. Tamil Nadu	8	10	7
6. West Bengal	9	11	10
7. Andhra Pradesh	4	2	3
8. Karnataka	10	13	9
9. Kerala	3	7	4
10. Bihar	2	8	2
11. Madhya Pradesh	7	12	8
12. Orissa	1	1	1
13. Rajasthan	6	2	6
14. Uttar Pradesh	5	6	5

Source : Appendix 4.4

Coefficient of rank correlation between per capita income 1990-91 through 1992-93 and

Per capita tax shares (-) 0.90* (Significant at1% level)
Per capita grants (-) 0.30 (Not significant)
Per capita total transfers (-) 0.86* (Significant at 1% level)

(a) The degree of progressiveness in terms of ratio of per capita transfers to per capita income recommended by the Tenth Finance Commission is higher than that of the first Eight Finance Commissions taken together. The degree of progressivity has increased from (-0.77) to (-0.86). This is a highly significant change. Tenth Finance Commission was able to do better than all the first Eight Finance Commissions taken together.

(b) The degree of progressivity of tax devolutions is highly significant in the Tenth Finance Commission. It has increased from (-) 0.63 during the period of the first Eight Finance Commissions to (-) 0.90 in the Tenth Finance Commission. This will surely, reduce the gap in post- tax devolution between surplus and deficit States and provide for the fiscal disadvantages of backward States. It may also help in reducing inter-state disparities, though some time lag may be involved. The factors responsible for this are :

(i) Decline in the weightage to population from 80-90 per cent by the First Seven Finance Commissions to 20 per cent by the Tenth Finance Commission.

(ii) Distance criterion instead of inverse income criterion adopted by the Tenth Finance Commission increased the degree of progressivity and proved the grounds on which it was adopted by the Tenth Finance Commission.

(iii) Area adjusted and index of infrastructure, the two new sets of indicators of backwardness ,introduced by the Tenth Finance Commission also added to the degree of progressiveness achieved by the tax devolution.

(c) The degree of progressivity in grants-in-aid declined in the Tenth Finance Commission. It came down from (-)0.63 to (-)0.37 which appears to be a significant decline. Had this not occurred, the per capita financial transfers by the Tenth Finance Commission would have been still more progressive. Grants-in-aid remained a mere gap-fillers.

The important policy implications that emerge from the analysis are that grants-in-aid should play a better and significant role than performed so far, if inter-state economic disparities are to be reduced by the Finance Commissions. The degree of progressivity achieved by grants-in-aid is inadequate to redress the horizontal fiscal imbalances inherent in our country due to many reasons. Fiscal disadvantaged States must be brought at least to the minimum national level, so that residents living anywhere in India are able to enjoy comparable level of socio-economic services and not feel bitter by being citizens of backward States.

SECTION IV : A NOTE ON THE ELEVENTH FINANCE COMMISSION (EFC)

The report of The Eleventh Finance Commission (June 30, 2000) covers a period from 2001-2005. The major recommendations are summarized below[20] :

- A lumpsum provision of Rs .11,00 crore in the Central Budget 2000-01 for revenue grants to states.
- For the period of five years commencing from April, 2000. The total share of the States in the net proceeds of the Union taxes and duties would be 28%.
- In deciding the total quantum of devolution of share in Central taxes/duties to States and grants-in-aid to States, tax devolution and Plan/non-plan grants from the Center to the States should not exceed 37.5% of total Centers revenues, both tax and non-tax.
- Grants-in-Aid under Article 275 (1) of the Constitution, amounting to Rs. 35,359 crore during 2000-2005 to be provided to such States (15 States) which will have deficit non-plan revenue account even after the devolution of Central tax revenues, equal to the amount of deficits assessed during the period 2000-2005.
- In its Supplementary Report, the majority view has recommended monitorable fiscal reforms programmes for all the States. Fifteen per cent of the revenue deficit grants meant for 15 States during 2000-2005 and a matching contribution by the Central government be credited into an Incentive Fund from which fiscal performance based grants should be made available to all 25 States. Total amount of the Fund comprising of both parts is recommended at Rs. 10007.72 crore for the five year period to be apportioned at the rate of Rs. 2121.54 crore per annum.
- The grants for specific purposes like upgradation, special problems and local bodies, which remain

unutilized due to non-observance of conditionalities attached to the release of these grants may also be credited to the Incentive Fund during 2004-2005.

- For the purpose of drawing a State-specific monitorable fiscal reforms programmes a monitorable fiscal reforms programme aimed at reduction of revenue deficit of States is envisaged.
- Only 15% of the revenue deficit grant to which a State is entitled may be withheld and linked with the progress in performance. 85% of the revenue deficit grants are to be released to the relevant States without linking it to the performance under the monitorable fiscal reforms programmes.
- The monitorable programme should give equal weight to raising of revenue and control of expenditure.
- The incentive component is to be provided to all the States. The initial eligibility of a State has been worked out on the basis of the population as per the 1971 census.
- The amount will be available to a State in proportion to the level of performance in the implementation of the monitorable fiscal reforms programmes each year.
- If any State is unable to get the full amount initially earmarked for it in any year, such amount will not lapse but will continue to be available in subsequent years to the same State .During the first four years, no amount of this Fund earmarked for assistance / incentive to a State, would be transferred to another State. However, if any State is not able to draw the amount indicated on the basis of the performance of the first four years the undisbursed amount to a State would form part of the common pool and would be distributed to the performing States in the fifth year on a pro-rata basis in addition to the amount to which they are initially entitled to. The same would apply to the withheld portion of grants to cover non-plan revenue deficit. Every State irrespective of the assessed

deficit or not would be entitled to get the assistance on a pro-rata basis related to performance from the additions to the Fund. This additional entitlement can go up to 100% of their initial eligibility indicated for the State concerned.

- The withheld amount of grants releasable in 2004-2005 may be released to the concerned assessed State on the basis of a review of their performance. In case any amount remains unreleased in a State, it would be added to the Fund and would be available to the remaining States. The balance amount in the Fund at the end of 2005-2006 will lapse to the Central Government.
- A group designated as monitoring agency may be constituted by the Government of India for drawing up State-specific monitorable fiscal reforms programme for all the States in the context of the broad parameters suggested by the EFC and as accepted by the Government of India.
- In addition to the incentives for better performance, Central government may also consider the fiscal reform programmes linking assistance by way of extended ways and means advance and aditional open market borrowings. This facility would also be extended to all the State linked to monitorable fiscal reforms programme.

The criteria and relative weights for determining the inter-state shares out of the divisible pool comprising 28 per cent of the net proceeds of all shareable Union taxes and duties can be summarised as below :

Criterion	Relative weight (per cent)
1. Population	10.0
2. Income (Distance method)	62.5
3. Area	7.5
4. Index of infrastructure	7.5
5. Tax effort	5.0
6. Fiscal discipline	7.5

NOTES AND REFERENCES

1. Government of India : *Report of the First Finance Commission,* 1952, p. 8.
2. Government of India : *Report of the Second Finance Commission,* 1957, p. 40.
3. Rao Hemlata : Federal Fiscal Transfers : Objective and Criteria. In, Sinha, R.K. (ed.) *Central State Financial Relations in India,* Deep and Deep Publications, New Delhi, 1986, p. 39.
4. Sinha, R.K : Readjustment In India : Some Major Issues. In Sinha, R.K. (ed.). *Ibid,* p. 27.
5. Government of India : *Report of the Fifth Finance Commission,* 1969, p. 67.
6. Government of India : *Report of the Sixth Finance Commission,* 1973, p. 8.
7. Government of India : *Ibid,* p. 7.
8. Hanson, A.H : *The Process of Planning,* Oxford University Press, London, 1966, p. 351.
9. Sastry, M.L. and G.R. Reddy : *Centre-State Financial Relations,* Centre for Economic and Social Studies, Hyderabad, Concept Publishing Company, New Delhi, 1988, p. 16.
10. Government of India : *Report of the Sixth Finance Commission,* op. cit., p. 15.
11. Thakur Ramanand : *Finance Commissions and Centre-State Relations in India,* Deep and Deep publications, New Delhi, 1982, p. 126.
12. Government of India : *Report of the Second Finance Commission,* op.cit., p. 25.
13. Government of India : *Report of the First Finance Commission,* op.cit., p. 97.
14. To make data comparable with the study of plan grants this Table is in plan periods. There is difference in plan periods and Finance Commissions periods.
15. Guhan, S. : Flawed Devolution Scheme, *Economic and Political Weekly,* June 9, 1990, pp. 1269-1274.
16. Thammaiah, G. : Second Report of the Ninth Finance Commission : Manipulated Normative Approach. In Shandilya (ed.) *Centre-State Financial Relations in India,* Deep and Deep Publications, New Delhi, 1994, p. 83.
17. Reserve Bank of India : *Report of the Tenth Finance Commission - A Summary, Reserve Bank of India Bulletin,* Jan-February, 1996; pp. 36-37.

18. Government of India : *Report of the Tenth Finance Commission*, p. 24.
19. Reserve Bank of India : *Report of the Tenth Finance Commission*, *op.cit.*, p. 40.
20. Government of India : *Report of the Eleventh Finance Commission*,

5

TRANSFER OF FINANCIAL RESOURCES THROUGH THE PLANNING COMMISSION AND THE CENTRAL MINISTRIES AND INTER-STATE DISPARITIES

The India we inherited was of ill-fed, ill-clothed, ill-housed and ill-educated people. Indian economy was stagnating and inter-regional disparities were growing. To reduce these inherited inter-state disparities planning was accepted as an effective instrument to restructure the economy. The Planning Commission was specifically given the role of equalising the levels of resources of the different States and their expenditures and to equalise the fiscal capacities of the States, so that all the States can at least provide minimum level of socio-economic services to their residents. The main task of the Planning Commission is to remove these disparities and transfer financial resources to the fiscally needed States. This chapter examines the role of plan assistance from the Planning Commission and discretionary grants from the Central Ministries to the States under Article 282 of the Constitution. Plan assistance will cover both grants under Article 282 and loans under Article 293 of the Constitution. In this context the chapter has been divided into two sections :

I. The Role of the Planning Commission.

II. The Role of Central Ministries.

SECTION I : THE ROLE OF PLANNING COMMISSION

The role of the Planning Commission is analysed from the First to Seventh Five Year Plan, covering a period from 1951-52 to 1989-90. The gap between the various States can be narrowed by improving the infrastructure of the backward and financially weaker States. These States are handicapped from the point of view of economic growth. Undeveloped, underdeveloped and inadequate socio-economic services of the States were the background against which the Planning Commission was set up. The Planning Commission has transferred massive plan assistance to the States during the past our decades, with the objective of equalizing not only the benefits received by the residents of the different States but also achieving equality in sacrifices made by them in the form of taxes. The plan assistance injected in a State will influence the growth of the State. Therefore, the State wise allocation of plan assistance will influence the relative development of the States and their ranking in levels of development, and the pattern of inter-state disparities. It will either reduce them or accentuate them, but in no case will it be neutral. If the plan assistance is positively correlated to levels of development (SCR) and State Domestic Product it will definitely widen inter-state disparities. Both, the quantum of plan assistance and criteria of its allocation among States is important from the point of view of reduction in inter-state disparities. Absolute elimination of inter-state disparities is neither aimed at nor is it attainable. What the plan assistance must ensure is a minimum level of socio-economic services which is at least equal to the all-India average. This is practicable and attainable within a foreseeable time span.

The Constitutional directives in India make it binding to remove inter-state disparities in the country and to bring all the units in the federation to a national minimum level in respect of certain basic social and economic services. Equalisation of development between States is one of the important objective in a federation and this is the very purpose of transferring resources from the Union to the States.

It is the Planning Commission that determines the size of the plan, lays down priorities, decides the quantum of resources to be raised by the Central government and the States and the plan assistance to be given to the States. In taking all these decisions, priority must be given to deliberately chosen pattern of plan assistance which gives greater assistance to backward States to overcome their handicap of fiscal disadvantages, even though such a pattern may yield low economic returns in the short run. The backward States cannot be made to wait for the 'trickle down' effects of economic development to reach them in the due course of time.

It is not possible to equalize the levels of all the public services in all the States. The aim of plan assistance should be to provide at least minimum level of basic socio-economic services at the all-India average level. Equity has to be defined in terms of minimum level of services that the States should be capable of attaining and maintaining with reasonable tax burdens. It is in this light that the role of the Planning Commission has to be judged. Briefly stated the purpose of central plan assistance is :

1. To bridge the resource gap at the State level. There is a wide variation in the States' own resources. The States not having adequate financial capacities must be provided plan assistance on a progressive basis.
2. To reduce inter-state disparities through its pattern of plan assistance. Larger per capita plan assistance to backward States will definitely have an equalizing effect on socio-economic disparities among different States.
3. To coordinate the development efforts of the States in pursuance of the accepted plan objectives and priorities.

Thus, the primary function of Central plan assistance is to fill the gap between the States' own resources and the cost of the States' plan expenditure. The major items of States' own resources are :

1. Balances from current revenues : The wider and more elastic resource base of the richer advanced States enables them to have higher balance of current revenues. The Finance Commission reassesses these estimates, but does not scrutinize the budgets of surplus States. The backward States have meager surpluses or no surplus and they are covered by grants-in-aid under

Article 275. The value of these grants-in-aid is eroded by inflation and backward States suffer on this account.

2. Contributions of public enterprises : Current returns of public enterprises are a function of investments made in the earlier plans. The public enterprises in developed States are able to give higher returns on investments made in them and thus enhance their current revenue receipts.
3. Market and other institutional borrowings : The financial institutions are guided purely by considerations which impel them to invest in developed States where they expect to get higher rate of return.

Their main objection to investing in backward States is the low absorption capacity of the latter. This generates a vicious circle of low demand for and supply of funds from financial institutions in backward States and these States remain backward. The only way out is for the Planning Commission to come to their rescue and give them higher plan assistance.

4. Additional resource mobilisation : Often termed as tax efforts of the States, puts the backward States, having a lower tax base at a disadvantage. The advanced States having a greater degree of industrialisation and development have a wider and larger tax base. The backward States can in no way match the advanced States in additional resource mobilisation. This is the very reason that backward States should be given higher plan assistance to bring them at par with the developed States.

The size of the per capita plan outlays of backward States will depend a lot on the plan assistance that they receive from the Union governments. Per capita plan outlay is a summation of States' own resources and the per capita Central plan assistance received by it. Thus, the pattern and criteria of plan assistance has a very important role in reducing inter-state disparities.

As already stated plan assistance is provided to the States through grants and loans. These two components of plan assistance are significant Constitutional provision for transfer of funds from the Union to the States. Most of the grants under Article 282 are given on the advice of the Planning Commission.

State governments would not have bothered about the pattern of assistance, under which they got funds from the Union i.e. the grant-loan ratio of assistance, had all loans been productive to pay the principal and interest at the time of maturity or if there was an assurance that fresh loans would always exceed the sums due as repayment installments and interest on past loans.

Backward States, being at the lower level of development have to invest a larger part of their budgetary funds in developing their infrastructure and socio-economic services. Investments in these services are not immediately productive and do not enhance their current revenues. It is, therefore, of utmost importance that the less developed States get more budgetary transfers in non-repayable forms than the more developed States. The pattern and criteria of Plan assistance is very significant from the backward States' view-point. Higher the ratio of grants to loans, lower will be the debt servicing charges. Backward States can not afford to service huge debts.

For the purpose of examining the effect of Central assistance on reduction of inter-state disparities, the plan era has been divided into two periods :

1. Prior to the Fourth Five Year Plan, termed as adhoc approach (1951-52 to 1968-69).
2. From the Fourth Five Year Plan to Seventh Five Year Plan, termed as Gadgil approach (1969-70 to 1989-90).

The periodisation is necessary because the Fourth Five Year Plan made a point of departure to the then existing ad-hoc and schematic pattern of plan assistance. Pre-Fourth Five Year Plan Period : During this period the quantum of plan assistance was based on the size of the State plans[1]. State plan outlays were determined by the Planning Commission after consultations with individual States. The gap between plan outlays and the own resources of the States was filled through Central assistance.

The grant-loan component of total plan assistance for the State plans became clear after grants and loans in given under different schemes was decided and grant loan components in each State was determined. If the sum total fell short of the quantum of assistance intimated to the States, the balance was provided through a general loan, termed as miscellaneous development loan.

Different plan schemes had different patterns of assistance. The main aim was to prevent diversion of funds by the States and to ensure adherence of the States to schemes of national importance. The State governments were required to take permission of the Planning Commission before any diversion of funds, otherwise the State forfeited proportionately the right to the grant assistance admissible under the scheme. But if the State achieved the target of State plan outlay as a whole, it got back the forfeited assistance in the form of a miscellaneous development loan[2].

There were certain schemes for which Central assistance could not be diverted at all. For example, assistance given for programmes of agriculture and cooperation. In their diversion, the forfeited amount did not qualify even for a miscellaneous development loan. Under this type of the pattern of assistance, the grant-loan component of assistance was not clear to the States, until after the end of the plan. At the end of the Third Five Year Plan, there were about 150 patterns of assistance for State plan schemes, and 100 for Centrally sponsored schemes[3].

Thus, plan assistance was given on adhoc basis and the Planning Commission did not develop any definite criterion. State plan outlays were also not fixed on the basis of any known criteria. The criteria for determining the quantum and pattern of States' plan outlay were too numerous, diverse and conflicting to be of any significance. The grant-loan break up was not known till the plan was completed.

The main features of the pattern of assistance before the Fourth Five Year Plan can be summed up as follows :

(a) Plan outlay of the States was decided by the National Development Council.

(b) Plan outlay of the States was fixed first and the gap between plan outlay so fixed and the States' own resources was covered by Plan assistance. Thus, Plan assistance was a residuary and a gap filler.

(c) No set pattern of assistance was formulated by the Planning Commission. The grant-loan component of the plan assistance was determined on adhoc basis. Every scheme had its own pattern of assistance, resulting in numerous patterns of assistance, and varied criteria.

(d) Plan grants were given on matching principle and they were conditional grants. The funds given for a particular purpose could not be diverted.

(e) The ultimate grant-loan break-up had an element of mystery and was not known till the plan was completed.

(f) Not all schemes in the State plans were eligible for plan assistance.

(g) In assessing the needs and problems of the States, factors like population, area, levels of income and expenditure, availability of certain services *viz.*, roads, schools, hospitals, extent of commitments carried over from the previous plan, state of technical and administrative services available and commitments on large projects or special programmes were taken into consideration. How and why these criteria were selected and what weightage was given to each of them is not known. Thus, till the beginning of the Fourth Five Year Plan, no definite criteria existed for the determination of plan assistance. The absence of objective criteria for inter-state allocation of Plan assistance was admitted by the Planning Commission as quoted by Grewal (1975).

"The States' First Five Year Plan included projects/ programmes which were in progress before the commencement of planned economic development. A broad view was taken about the development efforts that were envisaged in the different States and after assessing the resources to be raised by individual States, the quantum of Central assistance was fixed for each State for the entire Plan period.... During the Second Plan, the quantum of Central assistance was not predetermined. It continued to change from year to year in the light of financial position of the States and the Centre and the requirements of projects taken up in both the States' as well as Central Sector.... The National Development Council, it may be mentioned, did not specifically consider the principles for allocation of Central assistance to States either in the Second or the Third Five Year Plan. The main emphasis had been on the principles which should govern the determination of the States' Plan outlays".[4]

To study the impact of plan outlays, plan assistance and States' own resources on inter-state disparities, coefficient of range, coefficient of variation, average index (all-States average = 100) and coefficient of rank correlation have been estimated [with respect to per capita income 1960-61 and levels of development (SCR)]. Inter-state disparities would be reduced if the coefficient of rank correlation is negative.

The analysis is carried out in per capita terms with respect to plan outlays, plan assistance, States' own resources and plan grants and loans inter-state.

Table 5.1 relates to per capita plan outlay of the States, prior to Fourth Five Year Plan. The coefficients of range and variation decreased from 0.68 to 0.39 and from 53 per cent to 23 per cent in the First Five Year Plan to the Annual plans respectively. This implies that the gap between the highest plan outlay State and the lowest plan outlay State decreased over the years, which signifies a reduction in inter-state disparities insofar as outlays are concerned.

Punjab, all throughout had the highest plan outlay. The State having the lowest per capita outlay has been different for the different plans. In the First Five Year Plan, Rajasthan had the lowest plan outlay; in the Second Five Year Plan, Uttar Pradesh, in the Third Five Year Plan Bihar and in the annual plans West Bengal had the lowest plan outlay. The average of aggregate per capita plan outlay is Rs. 257.

Table 5.1

Per Capita Plan Outlay (1951-52 through 1968-69)

(Rs.)

States	First Five Year Plan (1951-52 through 1955-56)	Second Five Year Plan (1956-57 through 1960-61)	Third Five Year Plan (1961-62 through 1965-66)	Annual Plans (1966-67) through (1968-69)	Aggregate per capita plan outlay (1951-52 through 1968-69)
1	2	3	4	5	6
1. Gujarat	58	76	108	84	326
2. Haryana	-	-	-	-	-
3. Maharashtra	37	57	103	83	280
4. Punjab	105[H]	87[H]	126[H]	90[H]	408[H]
5. Tamil Nadu	20[L]	57	98	71	246
6. West Bengal	54	48	80	39[L]	221
7. Andhra Pradesh	33	52	91	58	234
8. Karnataka	46	62	100	70	278
9. Kerala	31	49	101	73	254
10. Bihar	25	40	67[L]	40	172[L]
11. Madhya Pradesh	34	48	84	44	210
12. Orrisa	56	54	120	60	290
13. Rajasthan	20	57	98	71	246
14. Uttar Pradesh	25	32L	72	53	182
Average index	42	55	96	64	257
Coefficient of range	0.68	0.46	0.30	0.39	0.41
Coefficient of r variation	53%	25%	17%	25%	23%

Source : Sastry, M.L. and G.R. Reddy : *Centre State Financial Relations*, Centre for Economic and Social Studies, Hyderabad and Concept publishing Company, New Delhi, 1988, p. 184.

Notes : 1. Haryana State was not formed during this time period.

2. H- stands for the highest, and L- for the lowest.

The average index of aggregate per capita plan outlay of States is computed in Table 5.2 Col(2) and States' ranks have been given in Col (3). The emerging trends are :

The States having above average aggregate per capita plan outlay	:	Gujarat, Maharashtra, Punjab, Kerala and Orissa.
The States having below average aggregate per capita plan outlay	:	Tamil Nadu, West Bengal, Andhra Pradesh, Kerala, Bihar, Madhya Pradesh, Rajasthan and Uttar Pradesh.

Table 5.2

Average Index of Aggregate Per Capita Plan Outlay and Ranking of States Accordingly (1951-52 through 1968-69)

	States	Average index of aggregate per capita plan outlay	Ranks of States on the basis of Col.(2)
	1	2	3
1.	Gujarat	127	2
2.	Haryana	-	-
3.	Maharastra	109	4
4.	Punjab	159	1
5.	Tamil Nadu	96	7.5
6.	West Bengal	86	10
7.	Andhra Pradesh	91	9
8.	Karnataka	108	5
9.	Kerala	99	6
10.	Bihar	67	13
11.	Madhya Pradesh	82	11
12.	Orissa	113	3
13.	Rajasthan	96	7.5
14.	Uttar Pradesh	71	12
	Average Index	257=100	

Source : Table 5.1.

Note : Ranking of States according to per capita income 1960-61 is given in Appendix 1.1.

Coefficient of rank correlation between aggregate per capita plan outlay and

Per capita income 1960-61	+ 0.48	(Not significant)
Levels of development (SCR)	+ 0.59**	(Significant 5% level)

Except for Orissa, all the other backward States are below average in respect of per capita aggregate plan outlay.

The coefficient of rank correlation of aggregate per capita plan outlay with respect to per capita income is +0.48 and with respect to raking of States according to the levels of development (SCR) is +0.59. This implies that plan outlay was directly related to per capita income of States as well as the level of development. Per capita plan outlay has two components *i.e.*, per capita plan assistance and per capita own resources. Both seem to have made plan outlay regressive. To study their individual impact on this trend, they have to be segregated in per capita plan outlay of the States.

Table 5.3 relates to the per capita plan assistance from the period 1951-52 to 1968-69. The coefficient of range decreased from 0.59 in the First Five Year Plan to 0.54 in the Annual Plans. The overall coefficient of range was 0.40. This implies, closing of gap between advanced and backward States with respect to plan assistance. This is also bone out by the coefficients of variation. This trend would definitely reduce inter-state disparities.

In Table 5.4 average index of aggregate per capita Central assistance is computed and States' are ranked accordingly. The following trends are observed in per capita plan assistance to the States during this period.

The States receiving above average aggregate per capita plan assistance	:	Punjab, Kerala, Orissa and Rajasthan.
The States receiving below average aggregate per capita plan assistance	:	Gujarat, Maharashtra, Tamil Nadu, West Bengal, Andhra Pradesh, Bihar, Madhya Pradesh and Uttar Pradesh.
The States receiving average aggregate per capita plan assistance	:	Karnataka

Table 5.3

Per Capita Plan Assistance (1951-52 through 1968-69)

(Rs.)

States	First Five Year Plan	Second Five Year Plan	Third Five Year Plan	Annual Plans	Aggregate per capita plan assistance
1	2	3	4	5	6
1. Gujarat	19	26	50	31	126
2. Haryana	-	-	-	-	-
3. Maharastra	14	20	39	24 L	97L
4. Punjab	50H	67	38	72	227H
5. Tamil Nadu	14L	29	53	32	128
6. West Bengal	40	22	41	27	130
7. Andhra Pradesh	19	28	58	39	144
8. Karnataka	23	30	63	40	156
9. Kerala	24	68	45	80H	217
10. Bihar	19	44	19L	58	140
11. Madhya Pradesh	22	32	64	37	155
12. Orissa	39	74H	40	71	224
13. Rajasthan	36	31	74H	49	190
14. Uttar Pradesh	13L	17L	46	30	106
Average	26	38	48	45	157
Coefficient of rang	0.59	0.63	0.59	0.54	0.40
Coefficient of variation	44%	51%	28.54%	40%	27%

Source : Same as of table 5.1.

Note : H stands for the highest and L for the lowest.

The backward States, Bihar, Madhya Pradesh and Uttar Pradesh got below all States' aggregate average per capita plan assistance and were also below average in respect to aggregate plan outlay. Thus, plan assistance to these backward States is responsible for their slow growth and keeping them at the lower bottom in the levels of development (SCR).

Table 5.4

Average Index of Aggregate Per Capita Plan Assistance and Ranking of States Accordingly (1951-52 through 1968-69)

States	Average index of aggregate per capita plan assistance	Ranks of States on the basis of Col.(2)
1	2	3
1. Gujarat	81	11
2. Haryana	-	-
3. Maharastra	62	13
4. Punjab	145	1
5. Tamil Nadu	82	10
6. West Bengal	83	9
7. Andhra Pradesh	92	7
8. Karnataka	100	5
9. Kerala	139	3
10. Bihar	90	8
11. Madhya Pradesh	99	6
12. Orissa	144	2
13. Rajasthan	122	4
14. Uttar Pradesh	68	12
Average Index	157=100	

Source : Computed from table 5.3.

Note : Ranking of States according to per capita income 1960-61 given in appendix 1.1.

Coefficient of rank correlation between aggregate per capita plan assistance and

Per capita income 1960-61 (-)0.28 (Not significant)

Levels of development (SCR) (-)0.29 (Not significant)

The developed States Gujarat and Maharashtra also got below aggregate average plan assistance, but their aggregate plan outlay was above average. Surely, their own resources must have been large enough to compensate these States for lower plan assistance. Whereas the backward States are financially disadvantaged States and have lower resource base and hence require larger plan assistance. Punjab, has got above average aggregate plan assistance and its aggregate plan outlay is also above average. Punjab could also have managed on its own financial resources.

The coefficient of rank correlation with per capita income is (-)0.28 and with levels of development is (-)0.29. The negative coefficient implies that plan assistance allocation has followed a progressive trend and helped to supplement the inadequate resources of the backward States. But the degree of the negative coefficient is very low and insignificant. The degree of progressiveness is inadequate to provide for the relative financial disadvantages of backward States. May be, that is the reason for inter-state disparities still persisting.

Table 5.5 relates to the aggregate per capita own resources of the States, calculated as the difference between the aggregate per capita plan outlay and aggregate plan assistance. The coefficient of range is 0.72 which is high and indicates a wide gap in the resource base of advanced and backward States. A similar trend is indicated by the coefficient of variation. All the advanced States except West Bengal have an index above the average index and all the backward States have an index below the average. There is a clear divide between the resource base of the advanced and backward States, which the plan assistance should have eliminated in order to reduce inter-State disparities. The trends observed are :

The States having above average aggregate per capita own resources	:	Gujarat, Maharashtra, Punjab, Tamil Nadu and Karnataka.
The States having below average aggregate per capita own resources	:	West Bengal, Andhra Pradesh, Kerala, Bihar, Madhya Pradesh, Orissa, Rajasthan and Uttar Pradesh.

Gujarat has the highest index (200) which is twice the average. Bihar has the lowest index (32). Gujarat's index is six times that of Bihar. On comparative basis Bihar should have

Table 5.5

Aggregate Per Capita Plan Outlay and Plan Assistance and Aggregate Per Capita Own Resources and Ranking of States Accordingly (1951-52 through 1968-69)

(Rs.)

States	Aggregate per capita plan outlay	Aggregate per capita plan assistance	Aggregate per capita own resources	Ranks of States on the basis of Col.(4)
1	2	3	4	5
1. Gujarat	326	126	200[H]	1
2. Haryana	-	-	-	-
3. Maharastra	280	97[L]	183	2
4. Punjab	408[H]	227[H]	181	3
5. Tamil Nadu	246	128	118	5
6. West Bengal	221	130	91	6
7. Andhra Pradesh	243	144	90	7
8. Karnataka	278	156	122	4
9. Kerala	254	217	37	12
10. Bihar	172[L]	140	32[L]	13
11. Madhya Pradesh	210	155	55	11
12. Orissa	290	224	66	9
13. Rajasthan	246	190	56	10
14. Uttar Pradesh	182	106	76	8
Average	257=100	157=100	100	
Coefficient of rang	0.41	0.40	0.72	
Coefficient of Variation	23%	27%	54.6%	

Source : table 5.1 and table 5.3.

Notes : 1. [Col.(4)=Col(2)-Col.(3)].

2. H stands for the highest and L for the lowest.

Coefficient of rank correlation between per capita own resources and

Per capita income 1960-61 + 0.82* (Significant at 1% level)

Levels of development (SCR) + 0.79* (Significant at 1% level)

got at least six times more Plan assistance than Gujarat. Table 5.3 Col.(6) indicates that Gujarat had Rs. 126 and Bihar Rs. 140 aggregate per capita plan assistance from First Five Year Plan to Annual Plans. The average index is 81 for Gujarat and 90 for Bihar in table 5.4 col.(2). Thus, plan assistance has not supplemented the resource base of the backward States. The backward States on their own have not been able to mobilise average level of resources. But to demand at least minimum level (all-States average level) of services from the State governments the residents of the States should also contribute at least minimum average level of resources which they have not done, prior to the Fourth Five Year Plan.

The time involved in the reduction of inter-State disparities will be cut short if residents of India contribute at least all-India minimum level of per capita resources, no matter where they reside.

The coefficient of rank correlation with respect to per capita income (1960-61) is +0.82 and with level of development (SCR) it is +0.79. Both the coefficients are highly positive and statistically significant. The implication is very clear that own resources are directly and significantly related to per capita income and level of development. If inter-state disparities have to be removed, the first necessary condition is to supplement the weak resource base of the backward States by transfer of funds to these States. This will increase their per capita income also. Once the per capita income increases, the residents of backward States will have the financial capacity to contribute more towards the resource base of their respective States, which will be sufficient to improve their relative rank in the per capita income and level of development. The process will be self-cumulative and help to reduce inter-state disparities, with the narrowing of gap between advanced and backward States.

The entire capital assistance to the States is treated as loans, irrespective of the purpose for which it is utilised. Whereas Central government's expenditure for the same purpose is in the form of grants. For example, the entire expenditure on civil works of Central government is financed out of capital grants, whereas similar items of capital expenditure undertaken by the States is financed in the form of loans, which is subject to repayment with interest. The residents of the States, will be provided services for which they will have to pay interest. This will only add to the problem of backward States having poor resource base.

This pattern of assistance required immediate correction, which came in the form of Gadgil formula in the Fourth Five Year Plan. Fourth Five Year Plan to Seventh Five Year Plan : The share of each State in the plan assistance, since the Fourth Five Year Plan, is governed by the Gadgil formula. The Gadgil formula treats the plan outlays as a residuary factor to be decided by the States. The States, rather than the National Development Council works out the size of their plan after the quantum of plan assistance from the Planning Commission is decided. The States considering their own resources and their non-plan revenue surplus, fix the size of their plans.

All the plan assistance is not brought under the Gadgil formula. Only that part of the plan grants is allocated on the basis of Gadgil formula which is meant for the 'State Sector' of the States' plans. The method for distributing plan grants is brought out by Thimmaiah, while discussing 'Plan grants and Gadgil Formula'[5]. For the purpose of allocating plan grants, the plan schemes are divided into two categories :

1. 'State Sector' of the States' plans : These include some irrigation, power, education and health schemes. These are suggested and initiated by the State governments and need an approval from the Planning Commission.
2. 'Central Sector' or centrally sponsored schemes : Includes programmes of employment, drought-prone area development, etc. These schemes are suggested by the Planning Commission and sponsored by the Central Ministries, their costs are entirely met by the Central government, and once completed their maintenance is entrusted to the concerned State governments. Obviously these do not come under the Gadgil formula.

Thus, all the plan funds are not brought under the Gadgil formula. For instance, Rs. 9,900 crores were available for distribution among the States during the last four years of the Sixth Five Year Plan (from 1978-79 to 1981-82). It was decided by the National Development Council that only Rs. 6,200 crores were to be allocated among States on the basis of Gadgil formula. The balance was set apart for special category States, hill areas and special problem areas, and not added to the divisible pool. The plan assistance covered under Gadgil formula is distributed among the States on the following basis :

1. A lump sum amount is set apart for meeting the requirements of special category States which include Assam, Himachal Pradesh, Jammu and Kashmir, Manipur, Meghalaya, Nagaland, Sikkim and Tripura. The grant loan component of plan assistance for them is 90:10.
2. The balance of the plan assistance is distributed among the remaining fourteen States. On the following criteria :

Criteria	Weightage In the original formula	Per cent As modified by NDC in 1980 (Modified Gadgil formula)
1. Population	60	60
2. Per capita income below the national average	10	20
3. Per capita tax effort	10	10
4. Outlay on continuing irrigation and power projects	10	-
5. Special problems	10	10
	100	100

Before, adopting the modified Gadgil formula in 1980 a minor change was made in 1979. The amount of Rs. 2000 crores that was available to the States as a result of reduction in the outlays for Centrally sponsored schemes, was to be distributed to the States under Income Adjusted Total Population (IATP) method (*i.e.*, inverse of per capita income multiplied by total population)[6]. Thus, plan assistance is distributed on two different basis since 1979, (a) Old Gadgil Formula modified in 1980, (b) New Income Adjusted to Total Population (IATP).

Grants are also given to the needy States to fill the gap between the States' plan outlay as approved by the Planning Commission and the States own financial resources available for plan purposes.

The schematic grant-loan component of Plan assistance prior to the Fourth Plan was changed to 30:70 grant-loan component. Thus, plan assistance was determined independently of the size and structure of States' plan outlay. The subjective bias of the pattern of plan assistance prior to this was done away with. The cumbersome process of first forfeiting the States of their grants if they did not meet the required stipulated finance on their part and then providing them an escape route of miscellaneous development loans was closed. Now, outlays are earmarked under certain head or sub-heads of development and if these are not met there is a corresponding cut in plan assistance. The State governments have to reach the agreed figure of expenditure.

The major factor in the distribution of plan assistance inter-state is population. Population was assigned a high weightage on the assumption that infrastructure facilities are required in direct proportion to population. In the initial stages there was also some logic in continuing transfers for major irrigation and power projects. These projects, once started could not be left in-between. They needed completion at the earliest. The criterion of per capita State income below the national average was accepted as fair enough to be able to remove inter-state economic disparities. Tax effort was to introduce some incentives to the States to mobilise their own resources and reward self-help. The weightage attached to the criterion of special problems gave the Planning Commission some margin of discretion and brought in dynamism in plan assistance. Individual States might have to face certain uncalled for problems from time to time and no formula can suit the needs of States for all times. Therefore, some subjectivity was needed to cover the special needs of some States which might arise over the five years of the plan period.

Loans are given for projects which are of national importance and in accordance with the objectives of national planning. The State sector schemes and Centrally sponsored schemes are mainly financed through Central loans. The terms and conditions are decided by the Central government. The schemes generally are related to water supply, drainage and flood control. These projects are not self-liquidating. They do not yield enough financial returns to cover debt servicing and the repayment of loan itself. State governments have to borrow new loans to pay the old loans.

Thus, a State once in debt is always in debt. States keep borrowing from the Central government perpetually and keep repaying it in the form of interest. A small part of the gross loan is left with the States to carry on its developmental activities. Such plan assistance should not be in the form of loans, but in block grants or conditional grants. Loan assistance should be limited to self-liquidating, revenue yielding projects. The 70 per cent plan assistance in the form of loans, will in no way reduce inter-state disparities.

In order to verify the degree of equalisation present in the pattern of plan assistance from Fourth Five Year Plan to Seventh Five Year Plan, coefficients of rank correlation have been calculated between per capita income of the State and aggregate per capita plan outlay on the one hand and aggregate per capita plan assistance and aggregate per capita own resources on the other. The coefficients of rank correlation have also been worked out with respect to level of development (SCR).

Per capita plan outlay from Fourth Five Year Plan to Seventh Five Year Plan is given in table 5.6. Column(6) relates to the aggregate per capita plan outlay from 1969-70 to 1989-90, covering a period of two decades. The coefficient of range

Table 5.6

Per Capita Plan Outlay from Fourth Five Year Plan to Seventh Five Year Plan (1969-70 through 1989-90)

(Rs.)

States	Fourth Five Year Plan (1969-70 through 1973-74)	Fifth Five Year Plan (1974-75 through 1977-78)	Rolling Plan (1978-79 through 1979-80)	Sixth Five Year Plan (1980-81 through 1984-85)	Seventh Five Year Plan (1985-86) through (1989-90)	Aggregate per capita plan outlay (1969-70 through 1989-90)
1	2	3	4	5	6	7
1. Gujarat	204	303	121	1079	1760	3467
2. Haryana	358H	527	185H	1395H	2244H	4709H
3. Maharashtra	199	418	127	983	1672	3399
4. Punjab	316	671H	161	1164	1957	4269
5. Tamil Nadu	134	252	65	650	1188	2289
6. West Bengal	82L	253	86	641	756	1818
7. Andhra Pradesh	98	227	82	579	971	2007
8. Karnataka	128	302	84	610	942	2066
9. Kerala	156	244	69	607	825	1901
10. Bihar	85	206L	53L	461L	730L	1535
11. Madhya Pradesh	190	418	127	983	1672	3390
12. Orrisa	114	243	75	568	1024	2024
13. Rajasthan	120	238	85	590	876	1909
14. Uttar Pradesh	132	247	65	527	942	1913
Average index	165	325	99	774	1254	2621
Coefficient of Range	0.63	0.53	0.55	0.50	0.51	0.51
Coefficient of Variation	47%	40%	38%	35.8%	38.5%	37%

Source : Same as of table 5.1.

Note : 1. H- stands for the highest, and L- for the lowest.

has decreased from 0.63 in the Fourth Five Year Plan to 0.51 in the Seventh Five Year Plan and the overall disparity range is also 0.51. This implies the closing of gap in per capita plan outlay, only at the extreme ends, the highest and the lowest aggregate per capita outlay State. Even amongst the States the disparity has decreased as shown by the coefficient of variation which decreased from 47 per cent to 38.5 per cent, though marginal variations were found between the coefficient of range and coefficient of variation during the Rolling Plan Period. The average of aggregate per capita plan outlay is Rs. 2621. The average index of aggregate per capita outlay is worked out in Table 5.7 col.(2) and the ranking of States done accordingly in col.(3). The emerging trends in per capita plan outlay are :

The states having above average aggregate per capita plan outlay	:	Gujarat, Haryana, Maharashtra, Punjab and Madhya Pradesh.
The States having below average aggregate per capita plan outlay	:	Tamil Nadu, West Bengal, Andhra Pradesh, Karnataka, Kerala, Bihar, Orissa, Rajasthan and Uttar Pradesh.

The aggregate per capita plan outlay of backward States, except Madhya Pradesh, is below the average level. The highest index is of Haryana — 180, and the lowest is of Bihar — 59. The aggregate per capita plan outlay of an advanced State (Haryana) is three times that of Bihar. This will in no way lead to inter-State equalization of plan finances, which is a necessary condition for reduction of inter-state disparities. The coefficient of rank correlation with per capita average income (from 1990-91 to 1992-93) is +0.77 and with levels of envelopment (SCR) is +0.67. Both are positive and of a high degree. Thus, higher the per capita income of a State and/or higher the level of development greater is its per capita plan outlay. This clearly indicates that plan finances, which are a part of per capita outlay have been regressive and in no way will help to reduce inter-state disparities.

Table 5.8 relates to per capita plan assistance (from Fourth Five Year Plan to Seventh Five Year Plan). The coefficient of range has increased from 0.46 in the Fourth Five Year Plan to 0.66 in the Seventh Five Year Plan. In the Rolling Plans (1978-79 and 1979-80) it was as high as 0.83. Thus, the disparity range in per capita plan assistance is increasing over the years.. This has also been corroborated by the coefficient of variation. If any reduction in coefficient of range in per capita

Table 5.7

Average Index of Aggregate Per Capita Plan Outlay and Ranking of States Accordingly (1969-70 through 1989-90)

States	Average index of aggregate per capita plan outlay	Ranks of States on the basis of Col.(2)
1	2	3
1. Gujarat	132	3
2. Haryana	180	1
3. Maharastra	130	4
4. Punjab	163	2
5. Tamil Nadu	87	6
6. West Bengal	69	13
7. Andhra Pradesh	77	8
8. Karnataka	79	7
9. Kerala	72	12
10. Bihar	59	14
11. Madhya Pradesh	129	5
12. Orissa	77	9
13. Rajasthan	73	10
14. Uttar Pradesh	73	11
Average Index	2621=100	

Source : Computed from table 5.9 .

Note : Per capita average income 1990-91through 1992-93 is given in appendix 1.1.

Coefficient of rank correlation between aggregate per capita plan outlay and

Per capita average income 1990-91 through 1992-93
+ 0.77* (Significant at 1% level)

Levels of development (SCR)
+ 0.67* (Significant at 1% level)

Table 5.8

Per Capita Plan Assistance from Fourth Five Year Plan to Seventh Five Year Plan (1969-70 through 1989-90)

(Rs.)

States	Fourth Five Year Plan	Fifth Five Year Plan	Rolling Plan	Sixth Five Year Plan	Seventh Five Year Plan	Aggregate per capita plan assistance
1	2	3	4	5	6	7
1. Gujarat	58	71	30	200	310	669
2. Haryana	76	89	42	253	305	765
3. Maharashtra	47	60	29	188	285	609
4. Punjab	89	27[L]	204	279	894	1493
5. Tamil Nadu	48	67	25	184	300	624
6. West Bengal	48	62	28	160[L]	224[L]	522[L]
7. Andhra Pradesh	53	79	43	226	307	708
8. Karnataka	57	78	28L	174	237	574
9. Kerala	104[H]	34	214	448	963	1762
10. Bihar	76	33	209	330	759	1407
11. Madhya Pradesh	61	71	35	234	363	764
12. Orrisa	98	59	311	437[H]	1089[H]	1994[H]
13. Rajasthan	83	97	39	274	337	830
14. Uttar Pradesh	38[L]	80	36	208	326	688
Average index	67	65	91	256	478	958
Coefficient of Range	0.46	0.56	0.85	0.46	0.66	0.58
Coefficient of Variation	30%	31%	103%	34%	61%	49%

Source : Same as of table 5.1.

Note : 1. H- stands for the highest, and L- for the lowest.

plan outlay is noticed, it is due to the own resources of the States. The average of aggregate per capita plan assistance is Rs. 958.

In table 5.9 the average index is computed and States are ranked accordingly. The emerging trends in per capita plan assistance are :

The States having above average aggregate per capita plan assistance	: Punjab, Kerala, Bihar and Orissa.
The States having below average per capita plan assistance	: Gujarat, Haryana, Maharashtra, Tamil Nadu, West Bengal, Andhra Pradesh, Karnataka, Madhya Pradesh, Rajasthan and Uttar Pradesh.

Table 5.9

Average Index of Aggregate Per Capita Plan Assistance and Ranking of States Accordingly (1969-70 through 1989-90)

States	Average index of aggregate per capita plan assistance	Ranks of States on the basis of col.(2)
1	2	3
1. Gujarat	70	10
2. Haryana	80	6.5
3. Maharastra	64	12
4. Punjab	156	3
5. Tamil Nadu	65	11
6. West Bengal	54	14
7. Andhra Pradesh	74	8
8. Karnataka	60	13
9. Kerala	184	2
10. Bihar	147	4
11. Madhya Pradesh	80	6.5
12. Orissa	208	1
13. Rajasthan	87	5
14. Uttar Pradesh	72	9
Average Index	958=100	

Source : Computed from table 5.11.

Coefficient of rank correlation between aggregate per capita plan assistance and

Per capita average income 1990-91 through 1992-93 (-)0.36 (Not significant)

Levels of development (SCR) (-)0.35 (Not significant)

The backward States of Madhya Pradesh, Rajasthan and Uttar Pradesh got below average per capita plan assistance over a period of two decades. This, in no way can lead to reduction in inter-state disparities. Plan finances are meant to supplement the inadequate resources of backward States. Punjab, an advanced State, has third rank in the receipt of per capita plan assistance, while it had fourth rank in levels of development (SCR). Obviously it does not need this much plan assistance when the aim is reduction inter-state disparities.

The coefficient of rank correlation with respect to per capita income is (-)0.36 and with respect to levels of development (SCR) is (-)0.35. This indicates a progressive distribution of plan assistance among the States. But the degree of progressiveness is too small and is not adequate to cover the financial disadvantages of backward States.

To bring out the poor resource base of the backward States aggregate per capita own resources of the States are estimated in Table 5.10 col.(4). The coefficient of range is 0.98 which is very high. This is a clear indication of the existing inter-state disparities in resource base of the advanced and backward States and this also corroborated by the coefficient of variation. The average of aggregate per capita own resources is Rs. 1663. Average index of aggregate per capita own resources is computed in col.(5) and States ranked accordingly in col.(6). The States can be grouped such as :

The States having above average aggregate per capita own resources	:	Gujarat, Haryana, Punjab, Maharashtra and Madhya Pradesh.
The States having below average aggregate per capita own resources	:	West Bengal, Andhra Pradesh, Karnataka, Kerala, Bihar, Orissa, Rajasthan and Uttar Pradesh.
State on the margin	:	Tamil Nadu.

Haryana has contributed the highest own resources towards its plan outlay as compared to the other States. Orissa has contributed the lowest, on an average 1.8 per cent over a period of two decades.

Table 5.10

Aggregate Per Capita Plan Outlay and Plan Assistance and Aggregate Per Capita Own Resources and Ranking of States Accordingly (1969-70 through 1989-90)

States	Aggregate per capita plan outlay	Aggregate per capita plan assistance	Aggregate per capita own resources	Average Index of per capita own resources	Ranks in the basis of col.(5)
1	2	3	4	5	6
1. Gujarat	3467	669	2798	168	2.5
2. Haryana	4709[H]	765	3944[H]	237	1
3. Maharastra	3399	609	2790	168	2.5
4. Punjab	4269	1493	2776	167	4
5. Tamil Nadu	2289	624	1665	100	6
6. West Bengal	1818	522[L]	1296	78	8.5
7. Andhra Pradesh	2007	708	1299	78	8.5
8. Karnataka	2066	574	1492	90	7
9. Kerala	1901	1762	139	8	12.5
10. Bihar	1535[L]	1407	128	8	12.5
11. Madhya Pradesh	3390	764	2626	158	5
12. Orissa	2024	1994[H]	30[L]	1.8	14
13. Rajasthan	1909	830	1079	65	11
14. Uttar Pradesh	1913	688	1225	74	10
Average	2621	958	1663=100		
Coefficient of Range	0.51	0.58	0.98		
Coefficient of Variation	37%	49%	68%		

Notes : 1. Col.(4)=Col.(2)-Col(3).

2. H stands for the highest and L for the lowest.

Co-efficient of rank correlation between aggregate per capita own resources and

Per capita average income 1990-91 through 1992-93 + 0.82* (Significant at 1% level)

Levels of development (SCR) + 0.80* (Significant at 1% level)

The coefficient of rank correlation of aggregate per capita own resources with per capita income is +0.82 and with levels of development (SCR) it is +0.80. Thus, there is a very high positive correlation between own resources, per capita income and level of development. This is the crux of the problem and brings us back to the vicious circle already discussed. Backward States have low own resources so have a low per capita income and low level of development. Because they have a low per capita income and low level of development, they have low own resource base. Plan assistance in the form of grants-in-aid, should supplement the inadequate resource base of the backward States. Loans would only add to their problems by making them enter a debt trap, thus adding another vicious circle of debt to their plight.

Backward States can come out of this plight only if they are given a higher percentage of plan assistance in the form of grants and not loans. The Gadgil formula of 30 per cent grants and 70 loans should have been reverse in their case, 70 per cent grants and 30 per cent loans in order to remove inter-state disparities and bring adequate progressiveness in Central assistance. The quantum of Central assistance is no doubt important, but more important is the grant-loan component of the Central assistance.

Table 5.11 brings out the proportion of per capita grants to the per capita aggregate plan assistance and ranking of the States. The average of aggregate per capita grants is Rs. 287. The average index of aggregate per capita plan grants is computed in col.(4) and ranking of States done accordingly in col.(5).

The highest average index of aggregate per capita grants is of Orissa (208). Orissa has the lowest average index of aggregate per capita own resources (1.8). On that ground it needed the highest percentage of assistance in the form of grants as it does not have the repaying capacity.

Kerala has 184 as the average index of aggregate per capita grants and Punjab's index is 156. To reduce inter-state disparities, grants given to Punjab could have been allocated to some backward State. Punjab has the third rank in own resources and is fourth on the basis of levels of development (SCR). Similarly Uttar Pradesh with an index of 72 got half the per capita grants compared with Punjab. This type of regressive per capita grant component will not reduce inter-state disparities.

Table 5.11

Aggregate Per Capita Plan Outlay and Plan Assistance and Aggregate Per Capita Own Resources and Ranking of States Accordingly

(Rs.)

States	Aggregate per capita plan assistance (Rs.)	Percentage of grants in per capita aggregate plan assistance	Average index of per capita plan grants	Ranks of States on the basis of col.(4)
1	2	3	4	5
1. Gujarat	669	200	70	10
2. Haryana	765	229	80	6.5
3. Maharashtra	609	183	64	12
4. Punjab	1493	448	156	3
5. Tamil Nadu	624	187	65	11
6. West Bengal	522	157	55	14
7. Andhra Pradesh	708	212	74	8
8. Karnataka	574	172	60	13
9. Kerala	1762	529	184	2
10. Bihar	1407	422	147	4
11. Madhya Pradesh	764	229	80	6.5
12. Orrisa	1994	598	208	1
13. Rajasthan	830	249	87	5
14. Uttar Pradesh	688	206	72	9
Average	958	287		
Average index		287=100		

Note : 1. Percentage of grants in per capita plan assistance is 30 per cent since Fourth Five Year Plan.

The mild degree of progressiveness in per capita Central assistance is inadequate and does not meet the required degree of progressiveness for the reduction in inter-state disparities.

On the other hand taking out a small portion from the ocean alike resources of rich advanced States will not make much difference to them, whereas it might provide a great material help to the poor backward States. This may also not affect the quantum of the divisible pool of the Planning Commission. This only implies restructuring the pattern of plan assistance.

SECTION II : THE ROLE OF CENTRAL MINISTRIES (DISCRETIONARY TRANSFERS)

Discretionary transfers refer to the assistance provided by the Central Ministries of Government of India. The main features of these transfers are :

I. Non-Plan and Non-Statutory. The purpose for which they are given is non-plan in nature and on current revenue account. Since they are outside the purview of the Finance Commission, they are termed non-statutory.

II. Provided under Article 282 and Article 293. Article 282 relates to the provision of grants and Article 293 to the disbursements of loans. Grants are given to the States to meet natural calamities, development of handloom industries, improvement in the scales of pay of University and College teachers, etc.

The non-plan non-statutory grants can be grouped into four broad categories :

(a) Grants for schemes which by their very nature, have to be implemented by the States under Central control or supervision.

(b) Grants to assist States in carrying out schemes which fall within their executive control.

(c) Grants to meet a large liability which is either unforeseen or of an indeterminate magnitude.

(d) Grants paid in pursuance of an understanding or agreement between the Central government and a State.

Plan loans are given by the Planning Commission. The non-plan loans were not in the terms of reference of any of the Finance Commissions. The Central Ministries have provided loans to the States for non-plan expenditure purposes.

III. Conditional and purpose-specific. Discretionary assistance to States is in non-formula form. Article 282 is concerned with providing residuary and marginal financial assistance to the States for unexpected purposes like natural calamities and flood Control.

Sarkaria Commission Report has brought out the nature of discretionary assistance to the States in following words[7] :

"The variety of purposes for which they are made by their very nature cannot be sufficiently anticipated by either the Finance Commission or the Planning Commission. Such transfers are purpose-specific and have to cater to the contingent problems which arise from time to time".

These transfers are necessary to meet unforeseen situations.

The relative importance of the four components of discretionary transfers; viz, schematic transfers; overdraft, and ways and means advances; small saving loans and assistance for meeting relief expenditure keeps changing over time as the situation warrants. Schematic transfers consist of three types of schemes :

Central plan schemes, centrally sponsored schemes and non-plan schemes proper. These schemes relate to subjects in the Central list, State list and the Concurrent lists of the Constitution.

Overdrafts, gap loans and ways and means advances are provided for overdraft facilities, loans for meeting gaps in resources and special accommodation loans respectively. The problems of unauthorized overdrafts arises either because the limits agreed to between the Reserve Bank of India and the State government are not strictly obeyed or because overdrafts are not cleared at the end of the stipulated period. Loans are given to the States to clear overdrafts and meet gaps in their resources on non-plan account. Overdrafts arise because of the administrative expenditure the States have to incur, increase in prices which the Finance Commission does not provide for. The situation regarding overdrafts is depicted by K.K. George in following words[8] :

"During the Fourth Plan Period, most of the States ran

into large overdrafts with the Reserve Bank of India which were cleared at the end of March 1972 by loans given by the Centre. Many States faced serious ways and means difficulties even in subsequent years. They would have been forced to resort again to heavy overdrafts, but for the loan given by the Centre to avoid overdrafts".

The Seventh Finance Commission recommended loans in the form of a share in small savings to meet the overall non-plan gaps. It recommended two-thirds of the net collection of small savings in each State to be given back to it as loans in perpetuity. From 1 April 2002 this share was raised to 100 per cent. As an incentive to make larger collection, the States were also offered half of every five per cent over and above the national average of net to gross collections. In addition, States also get non-plan grants for meeting half the expenditure on staff employed for popularising small savings.

This sharing formula adopted by the Union Government is regressive in nature. The high weightage given to collection serves only to perpetuate the inter-state disparities. This was the very basis on which the criterion of collection was discarded in the distribution of income tax inter-state.

Provision was made for famine relief while computing the normative non-plan revenue budgetary gaps for the purpose of determining the quantum of grants under Article 275 the Finance Commission, provide for famine relief. Central assistance from the Ministries is over and above famine relief. Relief for natural calamities is given irrespective of the budgetary position of the States or past accumulation of relief provisions with them. As far as natural calamities are concerned element of discretion is limited. No State would welcome a natural calamity just to get grant/loan from the Central Ministries.

The problem of overdrafts is self-created one by the States. They should learn to manage their financial affairs in a better way. Share from small savings is on the basis of collection and low per capita income of the backward States makes it regressive. But there is no element of discretion or bias by the Central Ministries. The problem is with schematic transfers, which tend to be discretionary. The percentage of schematic transfers in the transfer of financial resources from the Finance Commission and the Planning Commission is insignificant. Some flexibility is bound to be present in the allocation of funds from the Union, keeping in view the other national priorities and dynamic setting in which they have to be provided.

The discretionary transfers are mostly objected to by the States on the following grounds :

(a) They are not backed by any formula and a lot of political considerations weigh in giving these transfers.
(b) Equity consideration is missing in the allocation of these transfers.
(c) They increase the non-plan expenditure in the current period, therefore, Finance Commissions have to increase statutory grants in the following period.

These transfers reduce the divisible pool with the Union and hence reduce the allocation of financial transfers from statutory and plan assistance channels. The greater the percentage of discretionary transfers in the total transfers to the States from the Union, the lower will be the role of criteria based transfers, which can be allocated in such a pattern as to reduce inter-State disparities.

No matter, whatever the objections to discretionary channel of resource transfer to the States, they are necessary, to meet the unexpected needs of the States. No fiscal transfer mechanism can foresee and be complete and adequate to provide a provision for unexpected natural calamities before hand. Union must have some channel to meet the fiscal needs of the States.

The importance of discretionary transfers in the transfer of total resources through various agencies from the First Five Year Plan to the Sixth Five Year Plan covering a period from 1951-52 to 1984-85 is brought out in Appendix 5.1 In the First Five Year Plan discretionary transfers provided 7.3 per cent of the total resources, but this has increased to 20.5 per cent in the Sixth Five Year Plan. Discretionary transfers of such a magnitude having no criteria of distribution and no relationship with equity among States and reduction in inter-state disparities are bound to be regressive in nature and open to political bargaining.

The flow of per capita discretionary transfers from the Second Five Year Plan to Seventh Five Year Plan is given in Table 5.12. The average of aggregate per capita discretionary transfers is Rs. 950. The average index of aggregate per capita discretionary transfers is computed in table 5.13 and the States are ranked accordingly.

For testing discretionary transfers from the angle of equalising effect on the transfer of resources to the States, coefficient of rank correlation is estimated.

The coefficient of rank correlation with per capita average income (1990-91 through 1992-93) is +0.49 and with levels of development (SCR) it is +0.31.

Both the coefficients are positive implying lack of progressiveness in discretionary transfers. The absence of progressiveness is confirmed also by the coefficient of range which has varied between 0.54 (Third Five Year Plan) to 0.84 (Rolling Plans), (Table 5.12).

Punjab got the highest discretionary assistance and Madhya Pradesh the lowest as indicated by the average index of aggregate per capita discretionary transfers. On this basis States can be grouped as follows :

The States receiving above average aggregate per capita discretionary transfers	: Gujarat, Haryana, Punjab, West Bengal, Orissa and Rajasthan.
The States receiving below average aggregate per capita discretionary transfers	: Maharashtra, Tamil Nadu, Andhra Pradesh, Karnataka, Kerala, Bihar, Madhya Pradesh and Uttar Pradesh.

The backward States, Bihar, Madhya Pradesh and Uttar Pradesh have got discretionary assistance, below the average and one fails to understand, how an advanced State like Punjab got first rank even in discretionary transfers. But a closer look at the Table shows that Punjab got abnormally high

Table 5.12

Per Capita Discretionary Transfers (1956-57 through 1989-90)

(Rs.)

	Second five year plan	Third five year plan	Annual plans	Fourth five year plan	Fifth five year plan	Rolling plans	Sixth five year plan	Seventh five year plan	Aggregate per capita discretionary transfers
1	2	3	4	5	6	7	8	9	10
1. Gujarat	13	39	41	100	135	37	392	250	1007
2. Haryana	10	50	11	172	164	45	401	246	1107
3. Maharashtra	20	38	34	125	109	46	276	298	940
4. Punjab	10	50	67	99	293	36	843	721	2118[H]
5. Tamil Nadu	12	34	35	82	73	27	222	144	629
6. West Bengal	38	41	29	124	169	50	350	221	1022
7. Andhra Pradesh	20	45	57	124	83	36	198	150	713
8. Karnataka	7	23	46	140	108	32	271	248	875
9. Kerala	26	46	23	116	91	14	233	191	740
10. Bihar	37	28	45	42	116	28	215	154	665
11. Madhya Pradesh	23	30	39	25	91	20	172	173	573[L]
12. Orrisa	36	39	52	137	120	35	354	234	1015
13. Rajasthan	31	53	89	241	133	166	330	201	1245
14. Uttar Pradesh	13	16	25	46	111	30	230	181	652
Average Index	21	28	42	112	128	43	320	244	950
Coefficient of Range	0.69	0.54	0.78	0.81	0.60	0.84	0.66	0.67	0.57
Coefficient of Variation	50%	27%	45%	46%	41%	82%	50%	57%	40%

Source : George, K.K. : *Centre State Financial Flows and Inter-State Disparities in India*, School of Management Studies, Cochin, University of Cochin, 1982, p. 136.

Note : H- Stands for the highest and L- for the lowest.

discretionary transfers from the Fifth Five Year Plan (1973-74) onwards. May be the situation in Punjab demanded a high level of discretionary assistance. Rajasthan got the highest discretionary assistance in the Rolling Plan period of 1978-79 and 1979-80.

Table 5.13

Average Index of Aggregate Per Capita Discretionary Transfers and Ranking of States Accordingly (1956-57 through 1989-90)

States	Average index of aggregate per capita discretionary transfers	Ranks of States on the basis of col.(2)
1	2	3
1. Gujarat	106	6
2. Haryana	116	3
3. Maharastra	99	7
4. Punjab	223	1
5. Tamil Nadu	66	13
6. West Bengal	107	4
7. Andhra Pradesh	75	10
8. Karnataka	92	8
9. Kerala	78	9
10. Bihar	70	11
11. Madhya Pradesh	60	14
12. Orissa	107	5
13. Rajasthan	131	2
14. Uttar Pradesh	69	12
Average Index	950=100	

Source : Computed from table 5.12.

Coefficient of rank correlation between aggregate per capita discretionary transfers and

Per capita average income 1990-91 through 1992-93 + 0.49 (Not significant)

Levels of development (SCR) + 0.31 (Not significant)

Since these transfers are discretionary in nature and are for unexpected purposes, they are not bound to reduce inter-state disparities. Identification of the reasons for which they are given, does not specify inter-state equity in levels of development of States as one of them.

Central assistance was given to the States to reduce the glaring and persistent inter-state disparities in the backdrop of overall underdevelopment. The Directive Principles of State Policy enshrined in the Constitution require that the State should strive to minimise inequalities amongst groups of people residing in different areas[9].

Equalising the fiscal capacity of the States is a pre-requisite to the reduction in inter-state disparities. The criteria of Central assistance should take into consideration, the fiscal needs of the backward States and provide adequate resources to them.

During the first eighteen years of Planning, the backward States had suffered due to the absence of an objective formula to allocate the plan assistance. Even during the next two decades, these States continued to suffer inspite of the implementation of an objective Gadgil formula. No doubt, it did provide progressiveness to plan assistance, but not to an adequate extent. The own resources of the States, when added to plan assistance, made plan outlay of States all the more regressive. Advanced States had relatively higher own resources. The discretionary transfers from Central Ministries, by their very nature were purpose- specific and had nothing to do with reduction in inter-state disparities. Relief expenditure was provided irrespective of the financial status of the States. Share from small savings is regressive by nature as it is derived on the basis of collection of States. Schematic transfers are allocated on the will of the Central Ministries and again have nothing to do with equalising the financial status of States. The examination of the plan assistance and discretionary assistance from Central Ministries leaves us in no doubt, that they are regressive and iniquitous, allowing the glaring inter-state disparities to persist.

NOTES AND REFERENCES

1. Grewal, B.S. : *Centre-State Financial Relations in India,* Punjabi University, Patiala, 1975. p. 241.
2. *Ibid.*, p. 241.
3. *Ibid.*, p. 243.
4. *Ibid.*, p. 58.
5. Thimmaiah, G : *Burning issues in Centre-State Financial Relations,* Ashish Publishing House, New Delhi, 1985, pp. 98-119.
6. Sastry, M.L. and G.R. Reddy : *Centre-State Financial Relations,* Centre for Economic and Social Studies, Hyderabad and concept Publishing Company, New Delhi, 1988, p. 30.
7. Government of India : *Sarkaria Commission Report,* New Delhi, December, 1987, p. 279.
8. George, K.K. : *Centre-State Financial Flows and Inter-State Disparities in India,* School of Management Studies, Cochin, University, Cochin, 1982, p. 147.
9. Government of India : *Sarkaria Commission Report, op. cit.*

6

TRANSFER OF FINANCIAL RESOURCES FROM THE NON-BUDGETARY SOURCES AND INTER-STATE DISPARITIES

The transfer of financial resources from the Union Government to the States is from budgetary as well as non-budgetary sources. Statutory transfers through the Finance Commission and non-statutory transfers through the Planning Commission and Central Ministries constitute the budgetary sources. The non-budgetary sources are commercial banks[1] and all India financial institutions[2].

In this chapter the role of commercial banks and all India financial institutions has been examined in the context of reduction in inter-state disparities. Commercial banks and financial institutions can play a dominant role in promoting balanced development of the country acting as agencies mobilizing a substantial portion of the community's savings. Correction of inter-state disparities in banking development was one of the major objectives of nationalising fourteen major commercial banks in July, 1969.

With the nationalisation of the major banks and creation of public financial institutions, a large segment of the non-budgetary resources of the community came under the control of Union government. The allocation of non-budgetary resources to the States must also satisfy the norm of reduction in inter-state disparities.

The main argument advanced by the bank and non-banking financial institutions is that they do not have much demand for funds from the backward States. This is mainly due to the poor credit absorption capacity of backward States. A vicious circle of financial inadequacy exists in the backward States. Low level of development leads to low absorption capacity, which reduces both demand and supply of financial resources to these States, keeping their level of development at the low level. The flow of non-budgetary funds must break this impediment and take the backward States out of this financial trap.

It is true and an accepted fact that banks and non-bank financial institutions cannot ignore the profitability angle. Market oriented commercial banks, even if in the public sector, and other financial institutions do not accept the norm of reducing inter-state disparities as a test of their performance.

In India, public sector commercial banks and all India financial institutions have a dual role to play. They have to act, both as an investment agency providing term finance and participating in risk capital, and development institution sponsoring investment projects that are necessary for the overall development of the economy.

Performing both these functions at the same time, brings in the conflict between the principle of profitability and development priorities. This conflict has been indicated and brought out by Boskey in these words[3] :

> "The types of projects that a given bank prefers to finance reflect a particular constellation of many factors ... All 'bankable' projects are not necessarily economically important, nor is every economically important project necessarily 'bankable'. A development bank will not achieve its development objectives if it devotes its limited capital exclusively to 'bankable' projects, irrespective of their purpose; at the same time, as a bank..... it cannot afford regularly to ignore the financial aspects of proposals and thereby run the risk of failing to preserve its capital intact. Consequently a judicious blending of banking and development criteria has to be adopted and applied to the non-budgetary financial transfers."

Commercial banks were nationalised and host of financial institutions brought under Union government's control, to finance industry and agriculture in accordance with national objectives. Reduction in inter-state disparities was to be achieved by diverting funds so as to bring geographical dispersal of industries and investments to be channelised to priority sections specified by the union government. The priority sections are :

(a) Small borrowers in agriculture;

(b) Small scale industry, road and water transport;

(c) Retail trade and small business;

(d) Consumption credit to weaker sections (with certain limits and for specific need);

(e) Small housing loans to scheduled castes/scheduled tribes and other weaker sections (not exceeding Rs. 5,000).

India has adopted the model of mixed economy, where the role of private sector is also very large. The Planning Commission has suggested that for the achievement of the private sectors objectives, it would be necessary, to guide and channelize the assistance by financial institutions in accordance with the priorities of private sector programmes as indicated in the plan[4].

Within the framework of plan priorities, capital must be put to most effective and optimum use. Public sector commercial banks and financial institutions have to examine the project from economic, technical, managerial, organizational, commercial and financial aspects. A privately owned commercial bank or financial institution is not likely to ignore the profitability of the projects as it gets its funds from the market and pays reasonable returns to its shareholders. But a public sector commercial bank and financial institution has to bring a compromise between profitability and national objectives to deploy funds in accordance with planning priorities laid down for the private sector investments.

The important role of public sector commercial banks and financial institutions is to regulate private investments in desired channels, by performing the functions which comprise of the following :

(a) Issuing of bonds and debentures with government guarantee;

(b) The public sale of securities from their portfolio acquired either through direct subscription or underwriting activity or both. They also acquire securities through the promotion of companies. Thus, they build up portfolios of industrial bonds and securities. The significance of sale of securities by banks is stressed by Boskey in these words :

> "Portfolio sales represent both the culmination and the beginning of a cycle of activities in which the bank participates as a developer, first, of securities and later of market for these securities once they have become seasoned"[5].

(c) Planning, establishing and managing industrial enterprises are a part of non-financial promotional activities carried out by financial institutions. The public sector commercial banks and financial institutions were created to provide direct finance or refinance to the projects desired by national priorities. Reduction in inter-state disparities is one of them. Working within the framework of planning, the allocation of non-budgetary resources from these institutions must break the vicious circle of financial inadequacy of backward states. These financial institutions draw basically from the same pool of the community's resources as budgetary finance. Households invest in commercial banks, Life Insurance Corporations, Unit Trust of India and General Insurance Corporations. Financial institutions draw from them and finance credit and make investments in projects and thus link savers and users of capital. Financial institutions help in promoting the process of capital formation by bringing together the supply of savings and the demand for the investible funds. They act as a 'go between' in the saving and investment mechanism.

Table 6.1 is related to per capita budgetary and non-budgetary transfers to the States from 1973 to 1985. Col.(2)

indicates the per capita budgetary transfers and col.(5) to col.(7) the per capita non-budgetary transfers from commercial banks, industrial development banks and National Bank for Agricultural and Rural Development (NABARD) respectively. Col.(8) relates to total per capita non-budgetary transfers while col.(9) to aggregate of per capita budgetary and non-budgetary transfers. Col.(10) brings out the percentage of per capita non-budgetary transfers to total transfers.

Maharashtra has received the highest percentage — 69 per cent of non-budgetary transfers in the total transfers to the State. Punjab has 64 per cent, followed by Haryana — 63 per cent. The backward State Bihar has the lowest percentage — 26 per cent of per capita non-budgetary transfers in its total per capita transfers.

Orissa has 20 per cent, Madhya Pradesh and Uttar Pradesh have a slightly higher percentage of 36 and 35 respectively.

The all States' average percentage is 49. All the backward States are below the average percentage. West Bengal, an advanced State also has below average percentage of per capita non-budgetary transfers to total per capita transfers i.e. 47 per cent.

Thus, higher the ranking of States in accordance with the levels of development (SCR), the greater the importance of per capita non-budgetary transfers to total per capita transfers.

Col.(3) and col.(4) bring out the per capita transfers of funds from Commercial banks in the form of per capita credit and investment respectively. The disparity range in per capita credit is 0.81. Maharashtra has the highest per capita credit — Rs. 1815 and Bihar has the lowest — Rs. 188.

The coefficient of range in per capita investment is only 0.31. The highest per capita investment is in Gujarat and Haryana — Rs. 170 and the lowest is in Bihar — Rs. 90.

The two important conclusions that emerge from the above analysis are :

(a) The coefficient of range of per capita investments is low as compared to that of per capita credit. The

Table 6.1

Per Capita Budgetary and Non-budgetary Transfers (1973-74 through 1984-85)

(Rs.)

State	Budgetary (net)	Commercial banks			Industrial Develop-ment Banks	NABARD	Non budgetary transfers transfers	Budgetary and non-budgetary budgetary (aggregate)	Percentage of non-budgetary to transfers
		Credit	Investment	Total					
1	2	3	4	5	6	7	8	9	10
1. Gujarat	1214	743	170^{H}	913	608^{H}	80	1601	2815	57
2. Haryana	1079	952	170^{H}	1122	387	336	1845	2924	63
3. Maharashtra	1125	1815^{H}	124	1939^{H}	489	83	2511^{H}	3636^{H}	69^{H}
4. Punjab	1209	1394	113	1507	355	340^{H}	2202	3411	64
5. Tamil Nadu	1049	803	99	902	359	59	1320	2369	56
6. West Bengal	1121	639	134	773	214	22^{L}	1009	2130	47
7. Andhra Pradesh	1116	605	96	701	247	120	1068	2184	49
8. Karnataka	955^{L}	778	103	881	398	100	1379	2334	59
9. Kerala	1089	740	153	893	204	61	1158	2247	5
10. Bihar	1102	88^{L}	90^{L}	278^{L}	65^{L}	52	395^{L}	1497^{L}	26
11. Madhya Pradesh	1101	307	94	401	132	82	615	1716	36
12. Orrisa	1565^{H}	257	125	382	181	77	640	2205	29^{L}
13. Rajasthan	1193	400	140	549	241	82	872	2065	42
14. Uttar Pradesh	1150	315	96	411	123	76	610	1760	35
Average	1148	703	122	832	286	112	1230	2378	49
Coefficient of Range	0.24	0.91	0.32	0.75	0.81	0.88	0.73	0.42	0.41
Coefficient of Variation	11%	63%	22%	53%	51%	85%	49%	25%	27%

Source : George, K.K. : *Centre State Financial Flows and Inter-State Disparities in India*, School of Management Studies, Cochin, University of Cochin, 1982, pp. 218-219.

Notes : 1. H- Stands for the highest and L- for the lowest; 2. Col.(8) = Col.(5) + Col.(6) and Col.(7); 3. Col.(9) = Col.(2) + Col.(8).

State wise investment allocations have been more progressive than credit distributed.

(b) Bihar, a poor backward State has received lowest per capita credit as well as lowest per capita investment. The fiscal disadvantage of Bihar seems to have hindered the flow of non-budgetary funds to the State.

But unless, Bihar gets more financial transfers relatively, it will not be able to come out of its financial trap. The same is true of other backward States. Had non-budgetary funds been poured into these States, their credit absorptive capacity would have increased. The Planning Commission and the Reserve Bank of India have a definite say in the investment decisions of public sector commercial banks and all-India financial institutions. Therefore, the Union government cannot absolve itself of perpetuating inter-state disparities, by regressive allocation of non-budgetary funds.

(c) The coefficient of range in the transfer of funds from Industrial Development Banks (IDBs) is 0.88, which is higher than that of commercial banks. Here also, Bihar has the lowest per capita funds allocated to the State — Rs. 65. Gujarat has the highest — Rs. 608.

The disparity range in case of National Bank for Agricultural and Rural Development (NABARD) is slightly lower — 0.88. Punjab has got the highest per capita funds — Rs. 340 and again Bihar has received the lowest — Rs. 52. Thus, Bihar has got minimum industrial and agricultural per capita allocation of non-budgetary transfers. Advanced States Gujarat, Haryana, Maharashtra and Punjab have received maximum non-budgetary transfers from one stream or the other.

The average index of per capita transfer of funds from commercial banks, industrial development banks, NABARD and total per capita non-budgetary transfers is computed in table 6.2 in col.(2), col.(3), col.(4) and col.(5). Respectively, the ranking of States is done in Col.(6). From the analysis of the table following trends emerge :

The average of per capita transfers of funds from commercial banks is Rs. 832.

Table 6.2

Aggregate Index of Per Capita Non-budgetary Transfers and Ranking of States (1973-74 through 1984-85)

States	Aggregate index of per capita transfers from commercial banks	Aggregate index of per capita transfers from industrial development banks	Aggregate index of per capita transfers from NABARD	Aggregate index of total per capita non-budgetary transfers	Ranks of States according to col.(5)
1	2	3	4	5	6
1. Gujarat	110	213 H	71	130	4
2. Haryana	135	135	300	150	3
3. Maharastra	233H	171	74	204H	1
4. Punjab	181	124	304H	179	2
5. Tamil Nadu	108	125	53	107	6
6. West Bengal	93	75	20L	82	9
7. Andhra Pradesh	84	86	107	87	8
8. Karnataka	106	139	89	112	5
9. Kerala	107	71	54	94	7
10. Bihar	33L	23L	46	32L	14
11. Madhya Pradesh	48	46	73	50	12.2
12. Orissa	46	63	69	52	11
13. Rajasthan	66	84	73	71	10
14. Uttar Pradesh	49	43	68	50	12.5
Average Index	832=100	286=100	112=100	1230=100	1163=100
Coefficient of Range	0.75	0.81	0.88	0.73	
Coefficient of Variation	53%	51%	85%	49%	

Source : Computed from table 6.1.

Note : Ranking of States according to average per capita income (1990-91 through 1992-93) is given in Appendix 1.1.

Co-efficient of rank correlation between aggregate per capita non-budgetary transfers and

Per capita average income 1990-91 through 1992-93 + 0.95* (Significant at 1% level)

Levels of development (SCR) + 0.80* (Significant at 1% level)

The States receiving above average per capita funds from the commercial banks :	Gujarat, Haryana, Maharashtra, Punjab, Tamil Nadu, Karnataka, Kerala.
The States receiving below average per capita funds from the commercial banks :	West Bengal, Andhra Pradesh, Bihar, Madhya Pradesh, Orissa, Rajasthan and Uttar Pradesh

All the advanced States except West Bengal have received above average per capita funds from the commercial banks. All the backward States have received below average funds from the commercial banks. The middle level States Karnataka and Kerala have also received above average per capita funds from the commercial banks. Andhra Pradesh happens to be a below average State with respect to per capita funds.

The average index of Maharashtra — 233 is about seven times higher than that of Bihar — 33. This surely indicates regressive transfer of non-budgetary funds from commercial banks, specially after bank nationalisation.

The average for capita transfers of funds from industrial development banks is Rs. 286.

The States receiving above average per capita funds from the industrial banks :	Gujarat, Haryana, Maharashtra, Punjab, Tamil Nadu, Karnataka,
The States receiving below average per capita funds from the industrial development banks :	West Bengal, Andhra Pradesh, Kerala, Bihar, Madhya Pradesh, Orissa, Rajasthan and Uttar Pradesh.

All the advanced States except West Bengal have received above average per capita funds from industrial development banks. All the backward States are below average in respect to per capita transfers from industrial development banks. This is also regressive transfer of non-budgetary funds. The middle level States of Andhra Pradesh and Kerala are below the average while Karnataka happens to be an above average State insofar as per capita transfer of funds from industrial development banks are concerned.

The average index of Gujarat is 213 and it is nine times

higher than that of Bihar i.e. 23, which is the lowest. Thus, a host of financial institutions have distributed non-budgetary funds in a regressive manner and accentuated the already existing inter-state disparities. NABARD is basically working as an apex body for meeting the credit requirements of rural section in the form of production and investment credit to agricultural small scale and village industries, rural crafts, artisans and other allied economic activities. The bank gives long term assistance (upto 20 years) to the State governments for subscribing to the share capital of cooperative credit institutions. The average of per capita transfer of funds from NABARD is Rs. 112. The grouping of States on this basis is follows :

The States receiving above average per capita funds from NABARD	:	Haryana, Punjab, Andhra Pradesh
The States receiving below average per capita funds from NABARD	:	Gujarat, Maharashtra, Tamil Nadu, West Bengal, Karnataka, Kerala, Bihar, Madhya Pradesh, Orissa, Rajasthan and Uttar pradesh.

The two advanced States — Haryana and Punjab cornered the major portion of transfer of funds from NABARD. Andhra Pradesh is the only other State to receive above average per capita funds from NABARD. All other States are below average. Haryana has the highest average index — 300, which is fifteen times higher than that of West Bengal *i.e.*, 20, though West Bengal happens to be an advanced State. Bihar has the next lowest index — 46. The average index of Haryana is six times than that of Bihar. This again brings out the regressive nature of non-budgetary transfer of funds from financial institutions, in this case in agricultural/rural sector.

The average of total non-budgetary transfers is 1230.

The States receiving above average per capita non-budgetary transfers	:	Gujarat, Haryana, Maharashtra, Punjab, Tamil Nadu, Karnataka

The States receiving below average per capita non-budgetary transfers	:	West Bengal, Andhra Pradesh, Kerala, Bihar, Madhya Pradesh, Orissa, Rajasthan and Uttar Pradesh.

All the backward States are in the below average category, whereas all the advanced States except West Bengal are in the above average category. This has only perpetuated the existing inter-state disparities and made backward State relatively more fiscal disadvantaged.

The highest average index with respect to total non-budgetary transfers is of Maharashtra - 204 and it is six times more than that of Bihar - 32, which is the lowest. Bihar got minimum non-budgetary transfers from all the streams of non-budgetary funds.

In col.(6) States are ranked according to the average index of total per capita non-budgetary transfers. The coefficient of rank correlation between per capita non-budgetary transfers and average per capita income (1990-91 through 1992-93) is + 0.95, and with levels of development (SCR) is + 0.80. Both the coefficients are significantly positive and high.

The advanced States seem to have attracted the non-budgetary flow of funds due to the availability of infrastructural facilities and existing industrial centers. Even agricultural assistance from NABARD has gone to Haryana and Punjab. The market oriented financial institutions have not been able to allocate funds in accordance with national priority of reducing inter-state disparities.

Table 6.3 reflects the per capita deposits and advances of scheduled commercial banks of different States and per capita assistance disbursed by all-India financial institutions in 1994.

The analysis of the Table brings out the following trends :

(a) The per capita deposits and advances of the commercial banks are regressive in nature. The coefficient of range reflects wide variation and disparity in per capita deposits and advances.

(b) The coefficient of range is 0.75 in case of per capita deposits; 0.83 in case of per capita advances and 0.94

in case of per capita disbursement by all-India financial institutions.

Table 6.3

Per Capita Deposits and Advances of Scheduled Commercial Banks and Per Capita Assistance Disbursed by All-India Financial Institutions in 1994

(Rs.)

States	Per capita deposits of commercial banks	Per capita advances by commercial banks	Per capita assistance disbursed by All-India Financial Institutions
1	2	3	4
1. Gujarat	4448	2059	642
2. Haryana	3435	1727	268
3. Maharastra	8561H	5303H	700H
4. Punjab	7084	2978	223
5. Tamil Nadu	3657	3175	295
6. West Bengal	3903	1816	134
7. Andhra Pradesh	2379	1701	161
8. Karnataka	3242	2274	315
9. Kerala	4770	2115	115
10. Bihar	1365	493L	23L
11. Madhya Pradesh	1568	879	172
12. Orissa	1202L	733	145
13. Rajasthan	1821	896	213
14. Uttar Pradesh	2004	746	79
Average	3531	1921	249
Coefficient of Range	0.75	0.83	0.94

Source : Col.(2) and Col.(3) : *Center for Monitoring Indian Economy, Basic Statistics States,* Economic Intelligence Service, Bombay, Sept. 1994, table 14.3 and table 14.4.

Col.(4) : IDBI : *Report on Development Banking in India,* 1993-94, Industrial Bank of India, Bombay, p. 122.

Note : H- stand for the highest and L- for the lowest.

(c) The highest per capita advances and per capita disbursements from these non-budgetary sources are to Maharashtra and the lowest to Bihar. The per capita deposits are also the highest in Maharashtra and the lowest in Orissa.

(d) There are the inter-State variations at the extreme ends. To study the inter-state variations, average of per capita deposits and advances of commercial banks and of disbursements from all-India financial institutions have been computed and the States are grouped into two.

The average of per capita deposits of commercial banks is Rs. 3531.

The States having above average per capita deposits	:	Gujarat, Maharashtra, Punjab, Tamil Nadu, West Bengal, Kerala
The States having below average per capita deposits	:	Haryana, Andhra Pradesh, Karnataka, Bihar, Madhya Pradesh, Orissa, Rajasthan and Uttar Pradesh.

All the advanced States, except Haryana have above average per capita deposits. All the backward States have below average per capita deposits. This clearly brings out the fact that per capita deposits of commercial banks are a direct function of the levels of development (SCR). Higher the level of development of a State, higher are the per capita deposits in that State. This leads us to the very roots of the problem of inter-state disparities. The relative fiscal disadvantages of the backward States reflected by their relatively low per capita deposits, must be supplemented by diverting relatively more per capita advances to these poor backward States so that they can improve their order in relative levels of development as reflected by SCR.

The average of per capita advances made by commercial banks is Rs. 1921.

The States receiving above average per capita advances	:	Gujarat, Maharashtra, Punjab, Tamil Nadu, Karnataka, Kerala

The States receiving below average per capita advances	:	Haryana, West Bengal, Andhra Pradesh, Bihar, Madhya Pradesh, Orissa, Rajasthan and Uttar Pradesh.

All the advanced States, except Haryana have above average per capita advances from commercial banks, whereas, all the backward States have below average per capita advances from commercial banks. This is contrary to the desired pattern of per capita advances, if the goal is reduction in inter-state disparity. The advanced States mobilised more deposits so they got more advances. The backward States could mobilize only low per capita deposits. Therefore, they were given low per capita advances by the commercial banks. But this was the very trend existing in pre-nationalization bank era, which was objected to and banks were nationalized to change the pattern.

West Bengal, an advanced State had per capita deposits above the average level, but the per capita advances made to the State are below average. The deposits of West Bengal were diverted to other States. Karnataka on the other hand had below average per capita deposits, but it received above average per capita advances from commercial banks.

Haryana and Andhra Pradesh are below average in respect of both per capita deposits and advances. The examination of per capita advances made by commercial banks, makes one to conclude that they failed to act as corrective to the disequalising trends generated by the market forces in capital market, guided solely by profitability. They failed to transfer funds in a progressive manner required to reduce inter-state disparities. By utilising deposits of backward States in advanced States, where the rate of profitability was higher, they aggravated inter-State disparities. They failed to redeploy bank finance in reducing inter-state disparities.

The average of per capita disbursements from all-India financial institutions is Rs. 249.

The States receiving above average per capita disbursements	: Gujarat, Haryana, Maharashtra, Tamil Nadu, Karnataka,
The States receiving below average per capita disbursements	: Punjab, West Bengal, Andhra Pradesh, Kerala, Bihar, Madhya Pradesh, Orissa, Rajasthan and Uttar Pradesh.

All the advanced States, except Punjab and West Bengal, have received above average per capita disbursements from the financial institutions. Punjab being an agricultural State, is below average, but it received above average funds from NABARD. All the backward States received below average per capita disbursements from financial institutions. Thus financial institutions which were created to supplement the low resource base of backward States failed to do so. Rather, they perpetuated existing inter-State disparities by giving relatively more non-budgetary funds to advanced States.

In table 6.4 average indices of per capita deposits and advances from commercial banks and per capita assistance disbursed from all-India financial institutions are computed and ranking of the States done accordingly.

In respect of to average index of per capita deposits, Maharashtra has the highest index — 242 and Orissa the lowest — 34. Maharashtra had seven times more per capita deposits than that of Orissa. This clearly brings out the relatively low resource base of Orissa. The other backward States also have below average index. The sum total of the average index of the five backward States is 226, which is lower than that of Maharashtra — 242. Thus, the five backward States put together had per capita deposits, lower than that of Maharashtra. This is the very origin of inter-State disparities which were to be eliminated through progressive allocation of non-budgetary funds, which have so far been allocated on demand and supply basis. The impediment between low demand for funds from backward States due to their low absorptive capacity, motivating commercial banks and all-India financial institutions to divert the supply of funds to advanced States must be put to an end.

Table 6.4

Average Index of Per Capita Deposits and Advances of Scheduled Commercial Banks and Assistance Disbursed by All-India Financial Institutions and Ranking of States Accordingly (1994)

(Rs.)

States	Aggregate index of per capita deposits of commercial banks	Ranks of States according to col.(2)	Aggregate index of per capita advance of commercial banks	Ranks of States according to col.(4)	Average index of per capita assistance disbursed by All-India Financial Institutions	Ranks of States according to col.(6)
1	2	3	4	5	6	7
1. Gujarat	126	4	107	6	258	2
2. Haryana	97	7	90	8	108	5
3. Maharastra	242	1	276	1	281	1
4. Punjab	201	2	155	3	89	6
5. Tamil Nadu	104	6	165	2	118	4
6. West Bengal	110	5	94	7	54	11
7. Andhra Pradesh	67	9	88	9	65	10
8. Karnataka	92	8	118	4	126	3
9. Kerala	135	3	110	5	46	12
10. Bihar	39	13	26	14	9	14
11. Madhya Pradesh	44	12	46	11	59	8
12. Orissa	34	14	38	13	58	9
13. Rajasthan	52	11	47	10	85	7
14. Uttar Pradesh	57	10	39	12	32	13
Average index	3531=100		1921=100		249=100	

Source : Computed from table 6.3.

Coefficient of rank correlation between aggregate per capita income (1990 through 1992-93) and

Per capita deposits of commercial banks + 0.78* (Significant at 1% level)

Per capita advances of commercial banks + 0.82* (Significant at 1% level)

Per capita disbursements of all-India financial institution + 0.81* (Significant at 1% level)

Commercial banks should have allocated advances, in a progressive manner to supplement the poor deposit base of the backward States. Average index of per capita advances made by commercial banks again indicates that the highest index is of Maharashtra — 276 and the lowest is of Bihar — 26. Maharashtra received eleven times more per capita advances as compared to Bihar. This will in no way reduce inter-state disparities. It will only aggravate inter-state disparities by widening the gap between the advanced and backward States and make backward States more fiscally disadvantaged in comparison to rich advanced States. Their plight will be worsened and the impediment will become stronger. The average index of total per capita advances of five backward States is 196, which is lower than that of Maharashtra — 276. Thus put together, the five poor backward (BIMARU) States received relatively lower per capita advances than Maharashtra alone.

The average index of per capita disbursements from all-India financial institutions also shows that Maharashtra has the highest index — 281 and Bihar the lowest — 9. Maharashtra, an advanced State, received thirty-one times more per capita disbursements than that received by a poor backward State of Bihar. Thus, the flow of funds from all-India financial institutions aggravated the inter-state disparities.

The coefficients of rank correlation have been computed between average per capita income (1990-91 through 1992-93) and per capita deposits and per capita advances by commercial banks, as well as with the levels of development (SCR). All the coefficients are positive, indicating the regressive flow of non-budgetary funds with respect to per capita income and level of development. Higher the per capita income and the level of development, greater the flow of non-budgetary transfers (advances and disbursements) from commercial banks and all-India financial institutions.

The coefficient of rank correlation between per capita income and per capita deposits of commercial banks is +0.78 and with per capita advances it is +0.89. The disbursements from all-India financial institutions have +0.81 as the coefficient of rank correlation with per capita per income.

The per capita income reflects the low resource base and low level of development of the backward States thereby indicating the fiscal need of the States to come to all-India average level of development. Backward States, having low resource base, cannot be expected to come up to the all-India average level of development and increase their absorptive capacity. The vicious circle of demand and supply of non-budgetary funds must be broken by the Union government controlled commercial banks and financial institutions.

The coefficient of rank correlation between per capita deposits and per capita advances of commercial banks is positive + 0.88. This clearly brings out the regressive flow of fund from commercial banks. Advances have been poured into higher deposit States. This pattern of advances is similar to the collection criterion adopted for inter-State allocation of income tax which was rejected and discarded by the Finance Commissions as regressive in nature.

The commercial banks were nationalised specially to bring in dispersal of industries and allocating credit to backward States in order to reduce inter-state disparities. For this, the public sector banks should have financed projects and programmes in accordance with planning priorities and should not have been governed by market forces of demand and supply, in order to bring higher profits.

Table 6.5 reflects the credit deposit ratio of public sector banks in 1969, 1980 and 1994. The average of 1980 and 1994 is estimated and ranking of States done accordingly. The average index of average credit-deposit ratio is also computed.

Tamil Nadu has the highest credit-deposit ratio for all the three time periods viz. 133 per cent in 1969, 90 per cent in 1980 and 81 per cent in 1994. Thus, the State having highest credit-deposit ratio after bank nationalisation, happens to be the same as before bank nationalisation. Punjab had (only 27 per cent) the lowest credit-deposit ratio before nationalisation and still was the lowest in 1980 - 38 per cent. Uttar Pradesh happened to be lowest in 1994 - 30 per cent.

The coefficient of range was 0.66 in 1969 and declined to 0.41 in 1980, but again increased to 0.46 in 1995. Thus variations in credit-deposit ratio, at the extreme ends, declined after bank nationalization. Average of credit-deposit ratio in two time periods 1980 and 1994 is 57 per cent.

Table 6.5

Credit-Deposit Ratio of Public Sector Banks and Average Credit-Deposit Ratio and Average Index of Average Credit-Deposit Ratio and Ranking of States (1969, 1980, and 1994)

(Rs.)

States	Credit-deposit ratio of public sector banks in 1969	Credit-deposit ratio of public sector banks in 1980	Credit-deposit ratio of public sector banks in 1994	Average Credit-deposit ratio of 1980 and 1994	Average index of average Credit-deposit ratio	Ranks of States according to Col.(6)
1	2	3	4	5	6	7
1. Gujarat	49	52	46	49	86	11
2. Haryana	47	66	50	58	102	5
3. Maharastra	101	77	70	73	128	2
4. Punjab	27[L]	38	42	40	70	12
5. Tamil Nadu	133[H]	90	81	85	149	1
6. West Bengal	115	60	46	53	93	9
7. Andhra Pradesh	101	70	73	71	125	4
8. Karnataka	76	73	72	72	126	3
9. Kerala	66	68	41	54	95	8
10. Bihar	31	41	35	38	67	13
11. Madhya Pradesh	59	51	56	53	93	10
12. Orissa	52	57	60	58	102	6
13. Rajasthan	51	67	50	58	102	7
14. Uttar Pradesh	46	43	30	36	63	14
Average				57=100		
Coefficient of Range	0.66	0.41	0.46			

Source : Same as of table 6.3.

Note : 1. H stands for the highest and L for the lowest.

Co-efficient of rank correlation between aggregate per capita-deposit ratio and

Per capita average income (1990-91 through 1992-93) + 0.41 (Not significant)

Level of development (SCR) + 0.31 (Not significant)

The States having above average credit-deposit ratio	: Haryana, Maharashtra, Tamil Nadu, Andhra Pradesh, Karnataka, Orissa, Rajasthan
The States having below average credit-deposit ratio	: Gujarat, Punjab, West Bengal, Kerala, Bihar, Madhya Pradesh, and Uttar Pradesh.

Grouping of States on the basis of credit-deposit ratio clearly indicates the diversion of deposits from one State to another, especially from backward States viz., Bihar, Madhya Pradesh and Uttar Pradesh to advanced States viz., Haryana, Maharashtra and Tamil Nadu. Tamil Nadu has the highest index of credit-deposit ratio — 149, while Uttar Pradesh has the lowest — 63. The main losers are Punjab, Bihar and Uttar Pradesh. The other States *viz.*, Gujarat, West Bengal and Kerala are marginally below the average index. The main gainers of funds are Maharashtra, Tamil Nadu, Andhra Pradesh and Karnataka. Haryana, Orissa and Rajasthan are slightly above the average index. Though equilisation of credit- deposit ratio is no guarantee of reduction of inter-state disparities, but it definitely improves the financial base of the backward States and supplements their inadequate financial resources.

Some inter-state redistribution of non-budgetary funds can take place if developed advanced States get back less than what they have contributed in the form of deposits and poor backward States get back more than what they have been able to mobilise in the form of deposits.

The coefficient of rank correlation between average per capita income (1990-91 through 1992-93) and average credit-deposit ratio is + 0.41. The coefficient of rank correlation between average credit-deposit ratio and levels of development (SCR) is + 0.31. Thus, non-budgetary funds have not been deployed to the States where they are most urgently needed to break the vicious circle of fiscal disadvantages and raise the absorptive capacity of backward States by building up their socio-economic services at least to the average minimum all-States' level.

The solution does not lie in equalising credit-deposit ratios of States, but in reducing the incremental credit out of ever increasing deposits of the advanced States. Equalisation of credit-deposit ratios will merely imply that the richer advanced States will be entitled to the use of their bank deposits, the size of which will be relatively higher than that of backward States. There is a limit to the degree of equalisation, which is set by the compromise made in the conflicting criteria of profitability, required degree of industrial rate of growth, the required and desired degree of industrial dispersal and inherent availability of resources. The compromise has to be decided by the Union government and the Planning Commission within the framework of national priorities and reduction in inter-state disparities is one of them.

Commercial banks were nationalised and all-India financial institutions were set up mainly to finance industries. There are three most important factors responsible for any States' share in industrial assistance.

(a) Licenses issued for setting up industry in that area;

(b) Availability of entrepreneurs bringing viable project for assistance;

(c) State governments contribution in industrial development will give the available infrastructure facilities.

The licenses are granted mostly by the Union government, while commercial banks and financial institutions provide finance to these industries. By doing so they have only fulfilled the national priorities as indicated by the grant of licence. If this has not brought about the desired and required degree of dispersal of industries and reduced inter-State disparities, then commercial banks and financial institutions should not be held responsible.

Another argument of commercial banks and financial institutions is that they do not have much demand for funds from the backward States due to the poor absorption capacity of these States. This is said to be low because of the low level of development and lack of infrastructural facilities, implying the failure of the State governments. The States are caught in a web of low financial internal resource base, due to their lower per capita income and low level of development. The commercial banks and financial institutions can take the States out of the web by providing them relatively higher non-budgetary transfers. But the flow of non-budgetary funds has been regressive and has perpetuated the already existing inter-State disparities. The lack of entrepreneurs bringing in viable projects can be overcome by financial institutions by providing non-banking services also and bringing investment opportunities to the notice of domestic as well as foreign investors.

All-India financial institutions must undertake technical and economic surveys. The backward States need help here. Financial institutions have to point out the economic potentials of different States. This information should be easily and extensively available for the use of interested entrepreneurs. Financial institutions have to provide all the services required for making a project viable-promoting, issuing, underwriting and distribution of securities, in a package programme. This will help to allocate optimally the available non-budgetary financial transfers among different States and help to reduce inter-State disparities. The non-budgetary resources must pour into States where they are most urgently required for reduction in inter-state disparities.

NOTES AND REFERENCES

1. In 1990-91 total number of scheduled commercial banks operating in the country was 271. At present there are 28 nationalised banks. 14 major banks were nationalised on July 19, 1969 and 6 on April 15, 1980. State Bank of India with its 7 associate banks is at the top. Of the 271 scheduled commercial banks, 224 are in the public sector. Out of these 196 regional rural banks, which have been specially set up to increase the flow of credit to small borrowers in rural areas.
2. The expression 'All-India Financial Institutions' (IAFIs) refers to six all-India development banks, three specialised financial institutions and three investment institutions. These are as follows :

   AIDBs-All India Development Banks :

   IDBI Industrial Development Bank of India

   IFCI Industrial Finance Corporation of India

   ICICI Industrial Credit and Investment Corporation of India

SIDBI Small Industries Development Bank of India
IRBI Industrial Reconstruction Bank of India
SCICI State Credit and Investment Corporation of India
SFIs-Specialised Financial Institutions :
RCTC Risk Capital and Technology Finance Corporation
TDICI Technology Development and Information Company of India
TFCI Tourism Finance Corporation of India Investment Institutions
LIC Life Insurance Corporation
UTI Unit Trust of India
GIC General Insurance Corporation

3. Boskey Shirley : *Problems and Practices of Development Banks*, Baltimore, The John Hopkins Press, 1959, pp. 49-50 as quoted by Prabhu N. Singh in *Role of Development Banks in a Planned Economy*, Vikas Publishing House Pvt. Ltd., Delhi, Bombay, Bangalore, Kanpur, 1974, p. 65.
4. Prabhu N. Singh : *Role of Development Banks in a Planned Economy*, Vikas Publishing House Pvt. Ltd., Delhi, Bombay, Bangalore, Kanpur, 1974, p. 63.
5. Boskey Shirely : *Op. cit.*, p. 105.

7

CONCLUSIONS

Ever since Independence, the issue of inequalities in the level of development of various States has agitated economists, politicians and of course the people of the backward States.

Everyone living anywhere in India is entitled to equity in respect of development of facilities like roads, electrification, health and education by the very fact of being a citizen of this democracy. Their development is a matter of national commitment. The traditional 'trickle down' theory of development has failed to automatically solve the problem of backward States. The poorer States have not developed much despite considerable growth in the national economy.

The important question that immediately comes to one's mind is, as to what has the allocation of financial resources from the Union to the States achieved in regard to the reduction in inter-state socio-economic disparities? The disparity range in per capita income has increased over the period. It is high time that stock-taking of the pattern of allocation of resources by different agencies be done and accountability fixed for not adhering to the 'Directive Principles of State Policy' enshrined in our Constitution, which require that the government should strive to minimise inequalities amongst groups of people residing in different areas.

In a federation, inter-governmental financial transfers cannot be settled once for all. There are problems of tax-sharing and grants which require changes with the changes in national objectives. But one objective which has been there since the First Finance Commission is the removal of disparities in the inter-state socio-economic levels of development.

The problem of inter-state economic inequalities in some form or the other exists in almost all federations. An economic or functional approach to equitable distribution of national funds among the States should be guided mainly by the consideration of each according to its needs. States do not have equal fiscal capacities, therefore, the transfer of financial resources has to be deliberately and consciously, far greater to backward fiscal disadvantaged States, keeping in mind of course the tax- efforts of the different States and economy achieved in their expenditure by them. India, is a developing federation and wastage of financial resources is a luxury which it cannot afford. Therefore, it is of utmost importance that all States put in the maximum efforts to raise and conserve scarce financial resources. If the financial transfer scheme is based solely on equalisation of general need of the States and neglects the resource mobilisation efforts of the States, some of the backward States might enjoy the benefits of federal transfers without making any efforts of their own. Such States would live like parasites on the other States which are exploiting their financial capacities to go in for self help. They must get incentives for doing so by the Finance Commission. At the same time States with a perpetual begging bowl must be discouraged. No Finance Commission should subsidise inefficiency.

There are differences in the Constitutional sanction for the different forms of transfers. Taxes are shared among the States according to Articles 268, 269, 270 and 272 of the Constitution, whereas grants are effected under Article 275 and 282. Loans are granted under Article 293.

While transfers by way of tax sharing are effected solely by the Finance Commission, grants are disbursed by all the three agencies such as the Planning Commission, different ministries of the Government of India and the Finance Commission. Loans are sanctioned by the Planning Commission and the Ministry of Finance.

An analysis of the instruments of financial transfers from the Union Government to the States assumes importance not primarily because of the differences in Constitutional sanction, as stated above, or because of the different types of agencies through which they flow, but due to the impact of each form of transfer on the State budgets at a later stage. It is this impact of each form of transfer on the States' economy and on reduction in inter-state disparities, which needs evaluation. In this context the chapter is divided into two sections :

I. Conclusions of other studies on the evaluation of the criteria adopted by multi- agencies in reducing inter-state disparities.

II. Conclusions of the present study on federal fiscal transfers and inter-state disparities.

SECTION I : CONCLUSIONS OF OTHER STUDIES ON THE EVALUATION OF CRITERIA ADOPTED BY MULTI-AGENCIES

B.S. Grewal[1] emphasizes that the equalisation of social services at a minimum level, a necessary condition, is not sufficient for bringing about a reduction in inter-state economic disparities.

In this study, ranking of fourteen States is done according to three different indicators of economic and social development, *viz.*, the index of economic and social development, industrial development and per capita income (average 1962-63 to 1964-65) and state-wise distribution of Central assistance. An attempt is made to identify if there is any significant trend towards inter-state equalisation. The proportion of expenditure borne by Central assistance, in respect of backward states increased during the period under review (Second Five Year Plan to Fourth Five Year Plan), and is higher than that of the advanced seven States, *viz.*, Punjab, West Bengal, Gujarat, Maharashtra, Kerala, Tamil Nadu and Haryana. However, according to the author the difference between the collective share of each of the categories of States is small — nowhere it exceeds even one rupee. The maximum difference is of Rs. 1.44 during the period 1966-67 to 1968-69. This is only 13.2 per cent higher than the combined share of the advanced seven States during the same period. The margin is too small and inadequate in view of the fact that the average index of economic and social development of the backward seven States is only 56.9 per cent of that of the advanced seven States.

In order to further verify the degree of equalisation present in the approach of the Planning Commission, coefficients of rank correlation have been calculated between the index of annual per capita Central assistance and the index of economic and social development. For the period of three Annual Plans, the value of the coefficient of rank correlation was (-)0.284 and for the Fourth Five Year Plan it was (-)0.235. Both these values were statistically insignificant.

The Conclusion that emerged was that no objective criteria was evolved for the distribution of Central assistance, which was treated, till that date, as a 'gap-filler' between the States' own resources and their plan outlay However, actual allocation during this period reflected a favorable treatment accorded to less developed States.

G. Thimmaiah and Hemlata Rao (1986) have estimated rank correlation between Federal Financial transfers made on the recommendation of Finance Commission (Second to Seventh Finance Commission) and indicators of relative backwardness, *viz.*, per capita State Domestic Product at constant prices; poverty (percentage of people below the poverty line) and PQLI[2]. It was observed that most of the rank correlation coefficients were negative, thereby implying presence of some degree of equity. However, the authors felt that the values of these coefficients were not statistically significant. This would imply that the degree of equity had been very low. In other words, Finance Commissions' fiscal transfers had not been in favor of all the needy or less developed States.

The authors attributed this inequity in the distribution of Federl fiscal transfers to the defective methodology adopted by the past Finance Commissions, which was known as the "gap filling" approach.

The past seven Finance Commission never tried to estimate the relative true fiscal needs of the States' and recommended federal financial transfers accordingly. The estimated non-plan budgetary gap was equated with the fiscal need of a

State by all the past seven Finance Commissions. This was based on the assumption that the gap between estimated revenue and estimated expenditure represented the fiscal need of a State. This is open to dispute and the authors' view-point is that, the fiscal need of a State refers to its financial needs as dictated by economic factors, levels of development, disparities in the fiscal potential and levels of essential public services. Any transfer mechanism of resources must consider the three main objectives of federal financial transfers :

1. Meeting the fiscal needs of the States.
2. Reducing inter-state economic imbalances.
3. Providing incentives for efficient management of the finances.

The authors have suggested the fiscal needs approach,which should be followed by the Finance Commission, in order to achieve these objectives. Their suggested approach considers both revenue and expenditure sides of the State Governments' budgets and has three components which are as follows :

1. Revenue need of each State on account of inadequate revenue raising capacity.
2. General expenditure need in the field of 'police State' functions.
3. Specific expenditure needs for (a) maintaining capital assets, (b) equalsing "merit goods" and (c) improving urban civic services.

The sum-total of the fiscal needs on the revenue side and general as well as specific expenditure needs on the non-plan current expenditure side should be worked out. This sum-total amount in case of each State would be their true fiscal needs, which should be met by the Central government through financial transfers in the form of tax share and grants.

Ramanand Thakhur study aims at analysing a number of issues connected with the problem of financial transfers from the Union government to the States[3]. The main among them are :

1. Screening the shortcomings in the nature, composition and approach of all the Finance Commissions.

2. To study the problem of co-existence between the Planning Commission and the Finance Commission.
3. To suggest a growth oriented redistributive model of fiscal adjustment which would bring a compromise in the twin objectives : equity and efficiency.

Thus, the study focuses on restructuring the Planning process and reorienting the nature, composition, approach, working, criteria and pattern of devolution adopted by different Finance Commissions to improve significantly the climate of Union-State financial relations in India by maximization of growth and equitable distribution.

From the examination of the role of Finance Commissions (First to Seventh) and Planning Commission the following conclusions have been drawn in the study :

1. All the Finance Commissions have uniformly overlooked to emphasize the point that the whole divisible pool be treated as a unit.
2. As a consequence the fiscal redistributive impact generated by one progressive transfer has been contradicted by the transfer of other item on regressive criteria.
3. The criteria adopted so far have not brought about maximum balanced regional growth and therefore, needed modifications.
4. The quantum of the flow of resources from the Centre to the States has been increasing from 1951 onwards indicating heavy dependence of the States on the Centre which is not a healthy development. In order to change this trend adequate resource mobilisation at the State level is called for.
5. Finance Commission, though a statutory body has distributed only 25 per cent of the allocation whereas the magnitude of discretionary transfer disbursed by the Planning Commission and the Central Government have been increasing to the extent of about 75 per cent which has pushed the Indian federation towards centralisation.

6. Norms of licensing, investment and financing by the Central agencies operated adversely and inequitably to the poor States resulting in their slow growth. This needs improvement to reduce the inherent inter-state disparities.
7. The Gadgil formula of 30:70 grant loan ratio adopted uniformly for all the States by the Planning Commission had proved adverse and iniquitous to underdeveloped States, pushing them to the verge of financial insolvency and causing reverse flow of funds from the States to the Centre which is against all canons of Federal Finance.
8. Transfer of resources both by the Finance Commission and the Planning Commission have been iniquitous to the poorer states in comparison to the highest spectrum and the middle spectrum states and particularly to Bihar, which the author demonstrates in a few lines by analysing that the transfer of resources by the Sixth Finance Commission was not accordingly to the proportion of population. Bihar commanded 10.3 per cent of the total population of the country whereas it received 9.57 per cent. Bihar was refused grants under Article 275, four times by the First, Third, Fourth and Fifth Finance Commissions. The transfer of resources by the Finance Commissions from Centre to Bihar have invariably been lower than the national average in per capita terms. Similar was the case with some of the middle spectrum states like Uttar Pradesh, Tamil Nadu, Gujarat, Madhya Pradesh, Karnataka and lower spectrum states of Rajasthan. Similarly, the transfer of resources from the Planning Commission and the Central Government have been regressive. This regressivity of past transfers has been one of the important causes of the persistent regional imbalances, in availability of resources and service levels. If these inherited disparities are to be reduced, then the author suggests, that a high degree of progressivity must be introduced in inter-state allocation.

P.K. Bhargava in his paper on "Need for a Rationalized Basis of Transfer of Resources" has examined the criteria adopted by Finance Commission for distributing the proceeds of income tax (which is to be shared compulsorily) and Union duties of excise (sharing of which is only permissive) among the States inter-se[4]. According to him population has been the main criterion. Some weightage was also assigned to contribution/collection in determining the share of each State out of the divisible pool of income tax. According to the author, distribution on the basis of population does not necessarily have the desired redistributive effects because some of the relatively developed States are also more populous. For instance, the Fifth Finance Commission had fixed the percentage shares of Maharashtra and West Bengal in the divisible pool of income tax at 11.34 and 9.11 respectively as against 9.99 of Bihar and 7.09 of Madhya Pradesh.

It is suggested that the basic objective of transfer of resources from the Union to States is to reduce the level of existing disparities among the States. To attain this objective it is, therefore, desirable that the transfers, whether in the form of tax sharing or grants-in-aid should be made on the basis of per capita income of the States, as per capita income figures satisfactorily indicate the economic backwardness or progress of different States. The cost of providing services, will no doubt differ from State to State depending upon the price level. A State with a lower price level, will be able to provide services at a lower cost. But with a lower price level, the value of total output of that State would also be low, which will get reflected in its low per capita income. Thus, the cost of providing services is also reflected indirectly in the per capita income indices. Had the Finance Commissions made the transfers on the basis of per capita income, then according to the author, poorer states like Uttar Pradesh and Bihar would not have suffered and the recommendations of the Finance Commissions would not have widened the economic disparities.

For example the case of Uttar Pradesh amply proves the statement. The per capita income of Uttar Pradesh (at 1948-

49 prices) was Rs. 259.6 in 1950-51 which was the last year of the pre-planned period. This was about 5 per cent higher than that of the all India average per capita income of Rs. 247.5 during that year. Unfortunately, the State had continued to suffer. In 1975-76, the per capita income of the State was Rs. 781 as against the all-India average of Rs. 1005, which was 29 per cent below the all-India average.

The study points out that under the awards of the past Finance Commissions, the poor States have not received the highest per capita allocation of shared taxes and grants-in-aid. Punjab the third richest State in terms of per capita income, received the largest per capita assistance in 1960-61. Gujarat, the fourth richest State, also occupied the fourth position in per capita allocation arranged in descending order. The poorer states of Kerala, Madhya Pradesh, Rajasthan, Uttar Pradesh and Bihar were among the lowest recipients of per capita assistance. However, there was a slight improvement in the above situation in 1970-71 when the least per capita allocations were made to the richest states of Haryana and Punjab. But Bihar and Uttar Pradesh still received less than their due share.

Shailendra Singh in his study brought out the fact, that the most important principle of transference of resources can be none else but the financial balance of the different units at comparable level and efficiency of State services[5]. However, there were marked differences in the provision of State services as between the most advanced State and another, and in consequence the principle of "equal treatment" of equal individuals was openly violated. In particular, the poorer sections of population who benefit most by the provisions of the services by the State Governments received an unequal treatment solely upon the basis of residence. The seminar concluded that this was largely, if not entirely, due to certain in-built conceptual and methodological shortcomings which could be identified with the principles and procedures adopted by the Finance Commissions.

Hemlata Rao (1980) holds that the criteria adopted by Finance Commissions for devolution purposes, in no way helped them to achieve the much claimed objective of equalisation[6]. It was observed that the bulk of the federal fiscal transfers had been in favor of the relatively more developed States — identified on the basis of the composite index of development and per capita income. The coefficient of rank correlation and the regression analysis of federal fiscal transfers and the per capita income, revealed this trend. This analysis was from the second Five Year Plan to Fifth Five Year plan. The coefficients of rank correlation between population and per capita income were found to be insignificant which proved that population is an inadequate measure of levels of development and/or fiscal potential and hence a poor measure of general need. Correlation between population and per capita budgetary gap was negative and significant at 5 per cent level, which implied that States with low population in general had a higher per capita budgetary gap. This indicates that larger population did not measure even per capita budgetary need. Thus, population by itself is a poor indicator of need. A State like Maharashtra with a population of 5.04 crores is definitely not more backward than the State of Orissa with a population of 2.19 crores or Madhya Pradesh with 1.17 crores. The need for fiscal resources from the Centre varies from State to State on account of various other factors quite unconnected with the number of people living in a particular area. Population is neutral in equalising disparities and it should not be treated as a sole index of need. If undue weightage is given to this factor alone, it would make the federal fiscal transfer scheme regressive.

Collection/contribution criteria, was also found to be regressive as it would help the richer and more advanced States to get larger share of Central assistance. The socio-economic development factor was totally absent in the fifties. In gained importance only in the sixties. More recently, poverty ratio was introduced in the scheme of devolution. According to the study, this is an equalising criterion, and should be given more weightage.

An alternative method is suggested by the study, to achieve the objective of 'equity' and 'incentive'. In order to achieve equalisation objective, the federal fiscal transfers should be based on the fiscal need of the State which is expressed in the following manner :

$$N = R - E$$

N = estimated need

R = estimated revenue

E = estimated expenditure

This is based on the estimate of revenue that a State can raise on the basis of the fiscal potential available to it and estimate of expenditure on the basis of programme need, or various other determinants of expenditure.

D.T. Lakdwala (1986) in his paper on "Plan Finances in a Federal Economy" has examined the transfer of resources from the Centre to the States from the First Five Year Plan to the Sixth Five Year Plan and per capita distribution of plan assistance to States from 1969-74 and 1974-79[7].

The critical evaluation of Gadgil formula adopted since the Fourth Five Year Plan assistance to the States is put forth by the author, after going through the discussions in various studies, which can be summed up as follows :

1. The criteria of population (60 per cent weightage) and backwardness (10 per cent among states whose per capita income was less than the all India average) were generally accepted as fair.
2. The criterion of continuing irrigation and power project (10 per cent weightage) was accepted as logical after considering the two main arguments :
   (a) The states would get some incentives to continue with the projects beyond the plan period.
   (b) These projects, once, started must be completed, as a very large proportion of State resources were absorbed in these projects, for instance, more than 60 per cent of resources by four States, in the Fifth Plan period.
3. The criterion of tax effort (10 per cent weightage) come in for the severest criticism on three grounds :

(a) With the existing State tax structures, poor states stood to loose, relatively, when tax effort was judged as a proportion of revenue to the State income.

(b) The poor states would be doubly penalised as plan assistance, and States own resources determine the plan outlay, in which tax mobilisation enters as a powerful element.

(c) Between two States with equal tax efforts the State with lower population would stand to gain in per capita terms.

4. Discretionary assistance (10 per cent weightage) for special problems was generally accepted. In a dynamic setting, this was essential as no formula could suit the needs of all the states.

This study clearly points out that India is a country of many diverse States, and the inter-state inequalities are by no means particularly glaring. While States have been classified as developed and underdeveloped, most of the developed States have very large underdeveloped areas. States advanced in one respect are backward in another. Economic and social infrastructure of one type or another is lacking in many of them. It is, therefore, difficult to reconcile them to a highly progressive distribution of central plan transfers. Growth is dependent on many other factors than central plan assistance.

The weaknesses of the Indian fiscal federalism, have brought out the following irrtants in the centre-state financial relations as discussed by Dr. R.K. Sinha (1986)[8]. These have to be overcome, may be by constitutional amendments, if required.

The Planning Commission is mostly held guilty of entering into the areas which by right and definition belong to the Finance Commission. The Finance Commission, on the other hand, suffers from an inherent disability : its tenure is limited, and its operations cease once it has submitted its recommendations. It, cannot, therefore, take stock of any change in the existing situation, not even a most serious calamity like the cyclone that hit Tamil Nadu and Andhra Pradesh whereas a situation of this type needs urgent attention for fresh and immediate financial assistance. The Centre, therefore, will have no choice but to ask the Planning Commission to cope with the fresh situation. It is in this manner that the Planning Commission's scope has been widening so much so that the grants regulated by it far exceeded in magnitude than those by the Finance Commission. This creates an unwanted situation which demands constitutional remedies.

K.K. George paper (1986) — "Statutory transfers and Inter-State Disparities" forms part of the author's study on Centre-State financial flows and inter-state disparities in India[9]. This is a profound study of the instruments of federal financial transfers viz., tax sharing and grants. The practice of a few States getting large Central transfers by means of tax shares and others by means of grants which are just sufficient to fill their revenue gaps tends to be disequalising. The author further elaborates that, in fact the grants have been found to be inadequate even to plug the budgetary gaps, as their value gets eroded by price rise. While tax shares are expressed as percentages to the divisible pool, the grants are expressed in absolute amounts. While inflation increases the size of the divisible pool and consequently the tax shares, it widens the revenue gaps and the grants provided to some states by the Finance Commissions are barely enough to cover the gaps even at the time of sanction and become inadequate leading to reduction of plan outlays and unauthorised overdrafts. All the delicate balancing mechanisms carefully and painstakingly built by the Finance Commissions, thus, gets upset even before their reports get into prints by the continuous rise in prices for which no provision was made by any of the Finance Commissions till then.

I.S. Gulati states that "The Sixth Finance Commission, for instance, assumed price stability at 1971-72 level during the long eight years (1972-1979). But 60 per cent of the real worth of their grants was eroded even by 1974-75, the first year of the quin-quennium to which their award applied"[10].

Another connected problem covered by I.S. Gulati is regarding 'Revenue Surpluses'. In the case of some States, the Finance Commissions' awards just covered their non-plan budgetary deficits, by means of grants. But in the case of others, they left large surpluses. The author, after analysing the data on the non-plan revenue surpluses under the awards of the Finance Commissions (1966-1984), observed a positive and statistically significant correlation between the per capita non-plan budgetary surpluses left by the Finance Commissions and the per capita incomes. In fact, during the Fifth Five Year Plan, governed by the Sixth Finance Commissions award, correlation was perfect (the coefficient was +1). During the Sixth Five Year Plan, covered by the Seventh Finance Commission award, the value of the coefficient came down, but it was still positive and high (+0.521).

The outcome of this was that as a result of the surplus in non-plan revenue account, made possible largely by the inequitous tax-sharing, some of the States could aim at a larger size of their plans on the basis of higher resource mobilisation. The larger plans accelerated both their revenue raising capacity and the per capita non-plan revenue expenditure in the subsequent periods covered by the subsequent Finance Commissions.

The rank correlation coefficient between the per capita Fourth Plan outlay and the non-plan revenue expenditure during the Fifth Five Year Plan was +0.589. The coefficient for the Fifth Plan outlay and the non-plan expenditure during the Sixth Plan was also +0.59. Both the coefficients were significant at 5 per cent level. No Finance Commission has been able to break this vicious circle. It was further held that the provision of huge surpluses on non-plan account with a few States left the size of the divisible pool for the Central plan assistance reduced correspondingly. So, even if the Planning Commission were to bring more equitable transfers, the funds available for doing that would get reduced. This situation was inevitable as all the Finance Commissions depended primarily on tax sharing and not on grants. Besides none of the Finance Commission took into account the total pool of resources to be allotted among different States.

The author has summed up the analysis and also suggested modifications required in federal financial transfers.

The successive Finance Commissions did not have an integrated approach to the total statutory transfers. Their approach was ad-hoc and fragmented. They relied more on tax-sharing than on grants. Their approach was more judicial than economic. The criteria also varied from sharing of one tax to another. And even, the best of criterion evolved by them had barely touched the surface of the problem of ever-widening regional disparities.

The third agency in the financial transfer mechanism are financial institutions. The flow of institutional finance into a State is an important factor for increasing the pace of economic development. Institutional structure was built up in India by the Central Government to act as a corrective to reduce inter-state disparities. The disbursal of funds by these institutions has not been studied extensively from the angle of inter-state disparities. The two important elements of institutional finance are bank credit and assistance sanctioned by all India Financial Institutions.

M.L. Sastry and G.R. Reddy (1988) have examined the flow of funds from these two institutions. Their analysis starts from 1969 for banks credit, when major commercial banks were nationalised[11]. The position obtaining in 1969 has been compared with 1982 to assess as to how far the objective of balanced distribution of credit was achieved by them.

The analysis projected a high degree of concentration in the per capita distribution of advances of commercial banks. Credit-deposit ratio, another indication which can be used to analyse the regional imbalances in the distribution of credit in relation to the deposits mobilised in a State were found to be favorable to middle income States followed by high income States in the second phase and backward States in the last. While the credit deposit ratio in respect of group A and B States came down between 1969 and 1982, that of group C States improved. But the relative position of the States remained the same.

Assistance by term lending, the other important institutional source can be used as an effective means to lessen regional disparities in the distribution of investments and thereby generate income in the States. Location of industrial units is guided by consideration of locational advantage as well as the availability of infrastructural facilities, leading to the concentration of industrial units within the parameters of already developed centres. This had led to the channeling of institutional finance to those regions which were already developed. But with the greater emphasis of the government on the dispersal of industries, it was expected that there would be greater flow of institutional finance to backward regions than before, thus helping in the reduction of inter-State disparities. For this purpose the author has examined the flow of institutional finance and cumulative assistance rendered by some of the important all India financial institutions such as NABARD, LIC, IFCI, IDBI, ICICI and HUDCO. Out of these financial institutions, IFCI, IDBI and ICICI were solely engaged in financing industrial activity, while the investment pattern of LIC was more varied. NABARD and HUDCO served agricultural refinancing and housing finance respectively. On examination of the pattern of assistance, the author observed that the assistance rendered by almost all financial institutions was in favor of high income States followed by the middle income States. The author has attributed this to the poor response of the industry to set up units to these States. But whatever may be the reason for this emerging trend, it needed immediate rectification.

I.S. Gulati and K.K. George (1978) made an attempt to review inter-state flow of institutional finance, their regressive nature and the relative quantitative and distributive significance of this flow when compared to that of central budgetary transfers[12]. The study covered a period of seven years (1969-70 to 1975-76). The study first brought out the importance of institutional funds compared to the budgetary funds due to the following reasons :

1. Institutional finance accounted for 44 per cent of total finance (budgetary transfers and funds flowing into the States through the financial institutions).

2. Budgetary transfers cover the states' consumption expenditure, whereas almost all institutional funds go to finance production and investment. So, from the point of correcting the imbalances in inter-State development, the importance of the institutional funds is far greater than their ratio in total finance.

The author sums up in a few lines, by saying that, "to the extent the institutional finance fails to remove inter-state disparities, the role of central budgetary transfers for the reallocation of resources among the states, becomes much greater". Even budgetary transfers are somewhat regressive in their pattern of inter-state distribution. To make up for the pronounced regressiveness of institutional finance, the federal fiscal transfers would have to be very progressive in inter-state distribution. The greater the freedom with which the institutional finance is allowed to follow its present course, the larger would have to be the corrective role of the Central budgetary transfers. If the Central budgetary transfers were to be assigned a larger role to bring about an equitable inter-state distribution of resources, the greater would have to be the role of a statutory bodies like the Finance Commission.

I.S. Pawar (1994) in his paper "Centre-State Finance Relationship" outlines the terms of references to the Ninth Finance Commission in new perspective[13]. This was the first time that the Commission was asked to check the capital assets and requirements of States which were backward in the general administration. The Commission was further asked to look into the 'non-plan capital gaps' of the States and undertake a general review of the States debt position. The Commission was further required to adopt a normative approach in assessing the receipts and expenditures on the revenue account of the States and the Centre. The State which had gone in for better resource mobilisation was to be given incentives.

In principle there may be no objection to a normative approach being adopted by an independent body but by further specifying at the same time that the commission shall also "keep in view the special problems of each State, if any, and the special requirements of the Centre", the door was left open for the normative approach becoming highly subjective.

G. Thimmaiah (1994) in his paper "Second Report of the Ninth Finance Commission : Manipulated Normative Approach" holds that normative approach, howsoever objectively formulated, cannot be free from value judgment[14]. The choice of such norms as the average level of expenditure or the highest level of expenditure and the average tax-rate or the highest tax-rate involve invariably a value judgment. But it is possible to minimise subjective judgement in the formulation of such norms, by keeping the existing circumstances in mind. Such a normative approach should integrate all the three components of the Finance Commission's methodology *viz.*, reassessing the non-plan (or total) revenue account of the budgets of the State governments for the period covered by the recommendations of the Finance Commission; determination of the States' share of the divisible pool of taxes and its inter-se distribution across States; and other related issues referred to the Finance Commission by the Union government.

G. Thimmaiah critically evaluates this methodology adopted by the Ninth Finance Commission, if it achieved the primary objective of financial transfer to the States, that of reducing inter-state disparities. In the literature on fiscal federalism, the net fiscal needs approach has been developed to reduce inter-state disparities in the levels and quality of certain essential public services. In this 'net fiscal needs' approach, the most important objective is to equalise the normative level of essential public services across the States. The normative approach adopted by the Ninth Finance Commission has to be judged from this angle.

Ninth Finance Commission gave this a secondary importance, whereas reducing the revenue deficit by the year 1994-95 was given the primary importance. In order to do so, the Ninth Finance Commission modified the normative results. To achieve this never-achievable objective, the commission did all sorts of permutations and combinations of growth rates for different States; such that the projected post-devolution non-plan revenue budget for these States would show no deficit by 1994-95. The author holds, 'this is no normative approach'. It is not even the earlier 'gap-filling' approach. It is a hybrid of both.

S. Guhan (1995) in the his paper "Report of Tenth Finance Commission" suggested an alternative scheme to the Ninth Finance Commission's Scheme for financing deficits on the plan revenue account[15].

The study compared the criteria for horizontal sharing in the Tenth Finance Commission's Report with those recommended by its predecessors and concluded that the Tenth Finance Commission had taken a significant step forward in terms of logic, simplicity and equity in adopting identical criteria for the two shareable taxes, namely, income tax and basic excise duties and eliminated the contribution criterion in income-tax sharing. The Tenth Finance Commission felt that the important need is that the total transfer out of both kinds of taxes be adequate and progressive.

An analysis of progressivity in each of the criteria adopted by the Tenth Finance Commission, showed that (1) with reference to bench mark population shares, the distance criterion favored low income states *vis-à-vis* the high income ones, without hurting the middle income States too much; (2) the tax effort criterion helped the middle income States the most and (3) infrastructure criterion particularly, was in favor of low income States.

Thus, the dominant influence on progressivity of the distance criterion was tempered by the weight for population and modified in different directions by the other components. In the opinion of the author the Tenth Finance Commission could have arrived more or less at the same final result if it had opted for a simple and solid 'cocktail' of 40 per cent for population and 60 per cent for the distance criterion.

The Tenth Finance Commission failed to sort out the fiscally imprudent State (Andhra Pradesh) from the fiscally disadvantaged State (Bihar) by filling alike the residual revenue account gaps for both of them. As a result a middle income State like Andhra Pradesh with a per capita income 60 per cent higher and a per capita own tax revenue 3.4 times that of Bihar got a per capita deficit grant of Rs. 157.8 which was 2.7 times higher than that of Bihar's entitlement of Rs. 59.1.

Amaresh Bagchi (1995) in section I of his paper entitled "Tenets of Tenth Finance Commission : A Critique"[16] questions the efficacy of the Tenth Finance Commission in redressing the vertical and horizontal fiscal imbalances inherent in the distribution of powers and functions among the Centre and the States, and the disparate levels of income and development across regions.

Section II relates to vertical gap which in the opinion of the author is not easy to neutralise. For, after the revenues requirements of the different governments are assessed normatively, surpluses of the Centre may not match the needs of the States.

Section III deals with horizontal equalisation and sums up by stating that unfortunately, Finance Commissions in India have tended to be persuaded by consideration of progressivity as such rather than trying to see how the fiscal capacities can be equalised. By introducing a host of criteria, every Finance Commission has tried to appear more progressive than its predecessors.

By comparing the shares of States as estimated by Tenth Finance Commission by its formula and those the States would have got, if the Ninth Finance Commissions' criteria were applied, the author observed that the transfers under Tenth Finance Commission Scheme had reduced the share of high and low income States, by its new criteria, and there was a huge increase in that of the middle income and special category States. Excluding Bihar, all the other four States in the low income category lost by significant amounts. The gainers in the middle income States were Andhra Pradesh (Rs. 1903 crore), Karnataka (Rs. 1106 crore) and Kerala (Rs. 277 crore). Even if, one goes by the coefficient of variation, the Tenth Finance Commission's allocation is less progressive. The author concludes by asking two important questions : (a) If progressivity is to be aimed at as a goal in itself where does one stop? and (b) What is the optimum degree of progressivity?

SECTION II : CONCLUSIONS OF THE PRESENT STUDY

Coming first to the statutory transfers which come mainly from the Finance Commission, The main findings are :

- The transfers of financial resources from the Union government to the State governments from the Finance Commission have been progressive.
- The transfer of financial resources from the Tenth Finance Commission have been more progressive than from the first Eight Finance Commissions. The coefficient of rank correlation between per capita aggregate transfers and per capita average income (1990-91 through 1992-93) was(-) 0.86 in case of the Tenth Finance Commission as compared with (-) 0.77 for the First Eight Finance Commissions.
- The Finance Commission recommended grants-in-aid to the States showing deficit in their revenue budgets. Thus budgetary deficit was treated as fiscal need of the concerned State.

The terms of reference of the Ninth Finance Commission were significantly different from the earlier Commissions. For the first time the Ninth Finance Commission was asked to give recommendations on the capital assets and requirements of the States, which were backward in general administration, to look into the non-plan capital gaps of the States and review the debt position of the States and above all adopt a normative approach, rather than the gap-filling mechanism.

- This necessitated basic departure from the earlier Finance Commissions gap-filling approach. A normative assessment of the fiscal needs and fiscal capacities of the respective governments was made.
- The Ninth Finance Commission worked out a scheme for determining the plan deficit grant (deficits on plan revenue account), as the Ninth Finance Commission was required to study the plan component of the revenue budget of the States.
- Out of the two instruments of fiscal equalisation *viz.*, tax shares and grants-in-aid, the latter have been usually

more progressive than the former. However, an opposite trend has been observed during the time period of the Tenth Finance Commission. The devolution of tax shares are more progressive than grants-in-aid. The coefficient of rank correlation between the per capita income (1990-91 through 1992-93) and per capita tax shares is (-) 0.90 whereas it is (-) 0.37 with per capita grants.

Thus, the degree of progressivity of tax devolutions is highly significant in the Tenth Finance Commission. This will surely reduce the gap in post-tax devolution surplus and deficit States and provide for the fiscal disadvantages of backward States. It may also help in reducing inter-state disparities, though some time lag may be involved.

- This trend is brought about by the decline in the weightage assigned to population criterion in the allocation of divisible pool inter-se. According to the recommendations of all the Finance Commissions, prior to the Eighth Finance Commission, the weightage assigned to population for the inter-state allocation of income tax was about 80 to 90 per cent. It was cut down to 20 per cent by the Tenth Finance Commission. In the allocation of Union excise duty also, the weightage assigned to population was lowered from 44.44 per cent as given by the Eighth Finance Commission to 16.84 per cent by the Tenth Finance Commission.
- Distance criterion instead of inverse income criterion adopted by the Tenth Finance Commission also helped in increasing the degree of progressivity. The distance criterion gives weights in inverse proportion to the distance of the per capita income of the State in the reference period from that of the State with the highest per capita income.
- The grants-in-aid remained mere gap-fillers. The degree of progressivity achieved by grants-in-aid in case of the Tenth Finance Commission is inadequate to redress the horizontal fiscal imbalances inherent in our country.

> Had the grants-in-aid played a significant and better role than performed so far, the per capita financial transfers by the Tenth Finance Commission would have been still more progressive.

Insofar as the non-statutory transfers are concerned, the Planning Commission and the Central Ministries are the two important sources of financial transfers.

Undeveloped, underdeveloped and inadequate socio-economic services of the States were the background against which the Planning Commission was set up. The Planning Commission has transferred massive plan assistance to the States during the past four decades, with the objective of equalizing not only the benefits received by the residents of the different States but also for achieving equality in sacrifices made by them in the form of taxes. The plan assistance injected in a State would naturally influence the growth of the State.

The State-wise allocation of plan assistance will influence the relative development of the States and their ranking in levels of development and the pattern of inter-state disparities. If the plan assistance is positively related to the level of development and State Domestic Product it will definitely widen inter-state disparities.

Both, the quantum of plan assistance and criteria of its allocation among States is important from the point of view of reduction in inter-state disparities.

Absolute elimination of inter-state disparities is neither aimed at nor is it attainable. What the plan assistance must ensure is a minimum level of socio-economic services which tend to be equal to the all-India average. This is practicable and attainable within a short time span.

The main findings relating to the transfer of resources from the Planning Commission are given below :

Per capita plan outlay has two components (a) per capita plan assistance, (b) per capita own resources. Before, considering the two components, the relationship of per capita plan outlay with per capita income and level of development must be determined.

- The correlation between per capita plan outlay and levels of development is positive (0.59) and significant in the pre-Fourth Five Year Plan period. Implying thereby that as per capita outlay increases, the level of income and level of development also increases.
- The positive and direct relationship continued during the post-Fourth Five Year Plan period also. The coefficient of rank correlation is +0.77 for the per capita income (1990-91 through 1992-93) and +0.67 for the levels of development (SCR). Both are highly significant. Of the two components of plan outlay, the plan assistance did not bear any relationship with either per capita income or level of development. Insofar as the own resources of the States are concerned, they are significantly related to the per capita income and level of development. In the pre-Fourth Five Year Plan period, the coefficient of rank correlation is +0.87 with the per capita income and +0.79 with the levels of development.

In the post-Fourth Five Year Plan period it is +0.82 with the average per capita income and +0.80 with the levels of development. There is a very high positive correlation between own resources, per capita income and level of development. This is the crux of the problem. Backward States have low level of own resources as well as a low per capita income and low levels of development. Because they have a low per capita income and low level of development, they have low level of own resources. The vicious circle is complete. The impediment was to be overcome by making financial transfers from the Planning Commission adequately progressive.

The second source of non-statutory transfers are the Central Ministries and these transfers are usually called discretionary transfers.

- The coefficient of rank correlation between average per capita income and level of development with discretionary transfers are positive (+0.49 and +0.31 respectively) implying lack of progressiveness. Since these transfers are discretionary in nature and are for unexpected purposes, they are not bound to reduce inter-state disparities. Identification of the reasons for which they are given does not specify inter-state equity in levels of development.

- Equalising the fiscal capacity of the States is a pre-requisite to the reduction in inter-state disparities. The plan assistance and own resources of the States have made their plan outlay all the more regressive. The discretionary transfers from Central Ministries, by their very nature, were purpose-specific and had nothing to do with reduction in inter-state disparities. Thus, the non statutory transfer from the Planning Commission and Central Ministries were regressive allowing the glaring inter-state disparities to persist.

Apart from the above mentioned budgetary and non-budgetary transfers from the Union to the states, the latter also get funds from the financial institutions like commercial banks and other all-India financial institutions. With the nationalisation of the major banks and creation of public sector financial institutions, a large segment of the non-budgetary resources of the community is channelised through them, inter-se. The allocation of these non- budgetary resources to the States must also satisfy the norm of reduction in inter-state disparities.

- The coefficient of rank correlation between average per capita income and non-budgetary transfers is +0.85 and with levels of development it is +0.96. Both are highly significant. Implying thereby that the non-budgetary transfers have been regressive in nature.
- The low absorptive capacity of the backward States has motivated commercial banks and all-India financial institutions to divert the supply of funds to the advanced States, thereby perpetuating inter-state disparities, by giving relatively more non-budgetary funds to the advanced States.
- The non-budgetary funds have not been deployed in the States where they are most urgently needed to break the vicious circle of fiscal disadvantages and to

raise the absorptive capacity of the backward States by building up their socio-economic services. The non-budgetary funds must pour into States where they are most urgently required for reduction in inter-state disparities.

Now coming to the fiscal transfer mechanism which must ensure the minimum per capita expenditure required for providing floor level of services in each State.

- The States requiring deliberate transfer of proportionately more fiscal aid are all the backward States, viz., Bihar, Madhya Pradesh, Orissa, Rajasthan and Uttar Pradesh. West Bengal and Andhra Pradesh also fall in the above category of the States requiring deliberate transfer of proportionately more fiscal aid.
- The minimum additional funds required (fiscal need) in the short-run to provide floor (minimum) level of services in these States is the 'inescapable expenditure' to be provided to these States, if inter-state disparities are to be removed in the short-run. In the long run, the desirable level of service existing in the best performance State will bring out the fiscal need of the States.
- Such an attempt might yield low economic returns in the short-run, but it will deploy inadequate national resources where they are most urgently needed to reduce the inter-state disparities. Citizens of the backward States have a right, at least, to the average level of socio-economic services, if not to that of the most advanced State.

However, before transferring resources to the States according to their relative fiscal needs, their fiscal capacities should also be considered. The transfer of resources from the Union to the States should achieve balance between relative fiscal need and relative fiscal capacity of the States. This will bring in horizontal fiscal balance among the States. However, State governments do not have equal fiscal capacity, therefore, any transfer mechanism of resources from the Union to States must ensure the removal of inequalities in the fiscal capacity of the States. The main findings relating to fiscal capacity of the States are as follows :

- The general view-point is that with economic development of an economy, the absolute taxable capacity would increase, thereby, enlarging the base of the States own resources. Bihar was the only State in 1990-91, which had negative absolute fiscal capacity.
- Relative taxable capacity is nothing else but percentage of absolute taxable capacity to the Net State Domestic Product. The coefficient of rank correlation between relative taxable capacity and per capita income is positive +0.92 and is highly significant, implying, thereby a direct relationship between relative taxable capacity and per capita income.
- The coefficient of rank correlation between relative taxable capacity and composite index of development is +0.71. This also implies a direct relationship between relative taxable capacity and levels of development.
- But, then, one fails to understand, why Gujarat, Tamil Nadu, Kerala, Bihar, Rajasthan and Uttar Pradesh did not improve their relative fiscal capacity for a period of 3 decades. In 1970-71, Gujarat had the third rank and came down to fifth in 1990-91. Tamil Nadu had the fifth rank in relative taxable capacity in 1970-71, but it was eighth in 1990-91. These two States happen to be advanced States and have no valid reason for showing a declined performance in relative taxable capacity, specially when there is direct and positive relationship between relative taxable capacity and level of development.

Kerala is a middle level State, whereas Bihar, Rajasthan and Uttar Pradesh are backward States. They can be excused for not having improved their performance in relative taxable capacity. These States have not been able to overcome their inherent fiscal disadvantages. Such a situation after four decades (1952-1992) of transfer of resources from the Union to the

States cannot be lauded. It needs immediate attention and restructuring.

- The Effort Relative (ER) of the States (average index of the percentage of per capita tax of a State to its per capita income) must be at least equal to their Capacity Relative (CR) (average index of States per capita income). Under no circumstances should States have ER < CR. Such States must be identified as these are the States which have failed to mobilize additional resource according to their warranted capacity. The advanced States having ER < CR in the three years 1970- 71, 1980-81,1990-91 are Gujarat, Haryana, Punjab and West Bengal. Maharashtra, also had ER < CR for two years 1980-81 and 1990-91. Therefore, in 1990-91 all the advanced States except Tamil Nadu, had ER < CR. These States must be penalised for not collecting taxes according to what their warranted capacity.
- Tamil Nadu is the only advanced State which has ER > CR for the all the three years 1970-71, 1980-81 and 1990-91.
- All the middle level and backward States had ER > CR in 1990-91. Thus the backward States by and large have made more efforts on their own to raise resources more than what their capacity warranted and they must be given some incentives.
- 'Equity with incentive' should form the basis of restructuring federal fiscal transfers. Inefficiency of States in raising resources must not be subsidized at any cost. Wastage of scarce financial resources is a luxury which we can ill-afford.

Economic backwardness is a self-feeding process. A backward State in a backward country has a double disability. The economic backwardness of the country and that of the State interact and reinforce one another. A large proportion of population in these States lives under conditions that are unsatisfactory as compared to those prevailing elsewhere in India- conditions which can be defined sub-human in absolute terms. A State may be poor or rich, backward or advanced, underdeveloped or developed, in absolute terms, but its backwardness is relative to other States' development. Thus inter-state disparity can be reduced only when the financial transfers from the Finance Commission, the Planning Commission and Central Ministries and also by the Financial Institutions are in accordance with the relative fiscal capacities of States and their relative fiscal needs as indicated by the relative composite index of development. So far these financial transfers have not been able to make any dent on inter-state disparities.

NOTES AND REFERENCES

1. Grewal, B.S. : *Centre-State Financial Relations in India*; Punjabi University, Patiala, 1975.
2. G. Thimmaiah and Hemlata Rao, *op. cit.*, p. 38.
3. Thakur Ramanand; *Finance Commissions and Centre-State Relation in India*, Deep and Deep Publications, New Delhi, 1989.
4. Bhargava, P.K. "Need for a Rationalised Basis of Transfer of Resources". *Ibid.*, pp. 30-36.
5. Singh Shailendra (ed.) : *Union-State Financial Relations in India.* Sterling, New Delhi, 1977, pp. 69-82.
6. Hemlata Rao : "Federal Fiscal Transfers : Objective and Criteria" *in Centre State Financial Relations in India, edited* by Dr. R.K. Sinha, Deep and Deep Publications, New Delhi, 1986. pp. 36-52.
7. Lakdwala, D.T. : *op. cit.*, pp. 67-106.
8. Dr. R.K. Sinha. "Centre-State Finance Relation", *op. cit.*, pp. 179-222.
9. George, K.K., "Statutory Transfers and Inter-State Disparities". Sinha, R.K. (ed.) *Centre State Financial Relations in India*, Deep and Deep Publications, New Delhi, pp. 263-308.
10. Gulati, I.S. "Sixth Finance Commission award", *Economic and Political Weekly*, Bombay, February 1977.
11. Sastry M.L. and G.R. Reddy, *op. cit.*, pp. 48-55.
12. Gulati I.S. and George K.K. "Inter-State Redistribution Through Institutional Finance", *Economic and Political Weekly*, August 1978, pp. 1391-1403.
13. Pawar I.S. "Centre-State Financial Relationship". *op. cit.* pp. 176-186.

14. Thimmaiah, G. "Second Report of the Ninth Finance Commission : Manipulated Normative Approach". *Ibid*, pp. 63-87.
15. Guhan, S. "Report of Tenth Finance Commission", *Economic and Political Weekly*, April 22, 1995, pp. 877-886.
16. Bagchi Amaresh : "Tenets of Tenth Finance Commission : A Critique", *Economic and Political Weekly*, August 5-12, 1995, pp. 1985-1992.

APPENDICES

Appendix 1.1

Per Capita Income of States

(Rs.)

	1960-61	1970-71	1980-81	1990-91	1990-91 through 1992-93 Average	1996-97
1	2	3	4	5	6	7
Gujarat	362	827	2238	5850	2587	14875
Haryana		960	2601	7516	3380	16392
Maharashtra	409	838	2466	7598	3509	17666
Punjab	366	1244	3169	8423	3786	18008
Tamil Nadu	334	669	1541	4619	2029	11708
West Bengal	390	781	1645	4794	2020	9579
Andhra Pradesh	275	627	1659	4731	1829	10308
Karnataka	296	664	1644	4631	2090	10504
Kerala	259	662	1445	4032	1760	10309
Bihar	215	415	1007	2650	1618	4231
Madhya Pradesh	260	575	1240	4021	1615	7571
Orissa	216	575	1308	3596	1764	5893
Rajasthan	284	618	1429	4035	1150	8974
Uttar Pradesh	252	603	1296	3557	1600	6713
Average	301	718	1763	5004	2195	10909

Source : Col. (2) Government of India, Ministry of Finance, *Indian Economic Statistics,*1985.

Col. (3); col. (4); col.(5) from tables 3.11 to 3.14 col. (2).

Col. (6) from Centre for Monitoring Indian Economy Basic Statistics; States.Monthly Review of The Indian Economy. Economic Intelligence Service.Bombay.Sep1994.

Col. (7) from Statistical Abstract Punjab, 1999.

Note : Haryana did not exist in 1960-61 (therefore there are only 13 States).

Appendix 2.1

Physical Level of Services (Indicators of Development), 1971

Q	Gujarat	Haryana	Maharashtra	Punjab	Tamil Nadu	West Bengal	Andhra Pradesh	Karnataka	Kerala	Bihar	Madhya Pradesh	Orissa	Rajasthan	Uttar Pradesh
1.	827	960	838	1244	669	781	627	664	662	415	575	675	618	603
2.	108	70	167	52	75	97	29	62	42	31	27	27	26	24
3.	25.8	17.2	28.2	23.1	26.7	24.5	17.4	22.3	15.1	8.4	14.3	6.3	16.3	12.9
4.	10	34	13	39	17	28	12	07	24	25	10	30	12	30
5.	41	54	22	73	62	23	39	28	27	29	18	10	13	39
6.	14	44	08	72	43	26	27	13	20	29	09	19	14	40
7.	31.4	26.4	36.5	28.9	35.8	27.9	40.4	34.7	29.1	31.0	36.7	31.2	31.2	30.9
8.	61	75	52	85	48	48	58	52	53	43	42	34	66	50
9.	138	98	158	159	130	118	56	104	76	65	54	96	50	60
10.	26	90	38	52	91	09	34	38	100	12	12	08	12	21
11.	2.6	1.4	2.1	2.1	2.6	1.0	1.2	3.3	2.1	0.4	0.8	0.5	1.3	0.8
12.	124	60	151	133	95	99	68	95	282	41	42	47	64	48
13.	26.2	NA	12	37	20	11	26	17	15	12	06	15	13	14.6
14.	18	NA	12	37	20	11	26	17	15	12	06	15	13	12
15.	36	27	39	34	39	33	25	32	60	20	22	26	19	22
16.	28.8	32.2	16.9	42.4	28.9	41.5	17.2	14.6	22.8	29.7	12.9	12.0	16.3	29.4
17.	221	307	316	594	714	599	264	510	3106	670	162	366	146	382
18.	624	234	639	335	340	421	308	463	432	140	203	166	356	157

Appendix 2.2

Physical Level of Services (Indicators of Development), 1981

Q	Gujarat	Haryana	Mahara-shtra	Punjab	Tamil Nadu	West Bengal	Andhra Pradesh	Karna-taka	Kerala	Bihar	Madhya Pradesh	Orissa	Raja-sthan	Uttar Pradesh
1.	2238	2601	2466	3169	1541	1645	1659	1644	1445	1007	1240	1308	1429	1296
2.	369	347	539	256	295	264	130	172	132	152	88	108	108	132
3.	31.1	21.9	35.0	27.7	33.0	26.5	23.3	28.9	18.8	12.5	20.3	11.8	20.9	18.0
4.	11.7	51.7	14.4	61.3	20.7	37.0	14.3	7.7	31.2	34.0	10.8	42.7	13.6	42.7
5.	53	69	45	90	63	46	54	27	60	61	28	29	24	57
6.	24	62	10	88	44	36	34	16	13	36	15	26	20	57
7.	32.2	28.4	38.7	29.4	39.3	28.3	42.3	36.8	26.7	29.7	38.4	32.8	30.5	29.2
8.	72	85	59	89	56	56	61	63	74	49	50	55	63	54
9.	299	247	313	423	213	135	183	187	140	95	168	130	140	118
10.	100	100	100	100	100	65	98	96	100	65	78	62	70	69
11.	7.0	6.8	6.1	9.7	6.6	4.5	5.6	8.0	9.5	4.1	4.8	4.7	5.2	4.4
12.	150	61	152	133	98	99	68	94	292	40	43	49	64	48
13.	42.9	NA	65.4	127.9	65.7	60.1	43.0	51.0	45.9	26.2	8.1	30.7	25.4	21.5
14.	22	16	16	19	22	13	26	22	16	13	17	25	23	14
15.	44	36	47	41	47	41	30	38	70	26	28	34	24	27
16.	28.7	34.1	17.3	42.8	29.9	41.8	17.4	15.7	23.5	30.8	12.9	12.7	16.4	30.2
17.	323	555	595	955	111.9	640	487	595	2688	484	255	766	222	526
18.	3633	2188	2932	5133	1686	1029	1318	2425	2824	814	1370	623	1447	918

Note : NA stands for not available.

Appendix 2.3

Physical Level of Services (Indicators of Development), 1991

Q	Gujarat	Haryana	Maharashtra	Punjab	Tamil Nadu	West Bengal	Andhra Pradesh	Karnataka	Kerala	Bihar	Madhya Pradesh	Orissa	Rajasthan	Uttar Pradesh
1.	5850	7516	7598	8423	4619	4794	4731	4631	4032	2650	4021	3596	4035	3557
2.	899	721	1266	1064	848	340	329	487	492	305	360	360	266	302
3.	30.2	28.3	32.3	30.1	33.3	29.6	30.8	32.0	29.6	25.1	29.6	29.7	28.2	27.1
4.	11.5	65.6	21.9	77.9	60.0	62.4	19.7	13.3	34.4	36.1	22.1	30.7	23.8	60.9
5.	23.2	25.9	70.8	53.7	31.7	37.1	46.8	33.4	1.7	37.0	67.7	28.1	28.0	133.4
6.	26.8	72.7	11.3	92.7	42.5	35.8	39.1	20.4	14.8	43.5	22.1	30.7	23.8	60.9
7.	40.2	31.0	43.0	30.9	43.3	32.2	45.1	42.0	31.4	32.3	42.8	37.5	38.9	32.2
8.	88	88	71	93	67	72	68	68	83	59	54	62	76	67
9.	622.4	672.9	524.3	863.1	430.7	164.5	365.1	356.8	254.0	60.7	312.4	226.0	320.0	209.3
10.	100	100	100	100	99.9	69.4	100	100	100	68.4	84.1	64.6	74.9	71.4
11.	8.1	7.5	7.0	10.5	7.6	6.0	6.8	93	9.6	5.4	6.4	6.5	6.7	5.9
12.	150	61	152	133	98	99	68	94	292	40	43	119	64	48
13.	52.9	NA	62.7	134.5	81.9	61.4	49.6	98.6	56.7	30.5	16.9	35.2	32.0	23.9
14.	22	16	16	19	25	13	26	22	16	13	20	29	28	14
15.	60.9	55.3	63.0	57.3	63.7	57.7	45.1	55.9	90.6	38.5	43.4	48.5	38.8	41.7
16.	26.9	33.9	17.7	42.1	30.9	43.1	18.4	16.1	26.4	30.6	13.5	12.9	16.8	30.2
17.	382	587	673	1010	1284	649	500	659	3173	488	239	1254	184	625
18.	53.1	37.8	37.8	72.2	30.8	14.1	24.8	33.4	22.9	12.2	25.2	13.6	22.1	15.2

Note : NA stands for not available.

Appendix 3.1

Per Capita, Per Month and Annual Essential Consumption in 1973-74 at 1960-61 Prices

States	Rural			Urban		
	Prices index 1973-74 base 1960-61=100	PCPM EC 1973-74 (Rs.)	PCAEC 1973-74 (Rs.)	Price index 1973-74 base 1960-61=100	PCPM EC 1973-74 (Rs.)	PCAEC 1973-74 (Rs.)
Gujarat	248.56	47.10	562.20	246.01	60.08	721
Haryana	282.23	49.95	599.40	255.54	52.07	625
Maharashtra	283.01	50.47	605.60	240.34	58.64	704
Punjab	282.23	49.95	599.40	254.22	51.80	622
Tamil Nadu	246.57	45.09	541.10	239.96	54.34	652
West Bengal	277.92	54.49	653.90	242.71	54.69	656
Andhra Pradesh	244.54	41.71	500.50	250.50	55.11	661
Karnataka	283.46	47.24	566.90	266.53	57.87	694
Kerala	286.85	51.68	620.20	273.03	62.08	745
Bihar	334.55	57.68	692.20	273.23	60.29	723
Madhya Pradesh	316.62	50.20	603.40	276.48	63.65	764
Orissa	283.27	46.87	562.40	245.97	60.18	722
Rajasthan	291.86	50.96	611.50	268.64	60.77	729
Uttar Pradesh	306.93	48.92	587.00	270.80	56.81	682

Source : Government of India : Report of the expert group on Estimation of proportion and number of poor : perspective planning division, Planning Commission, New Delhi, July 1993 consumer price index for agricultural labour col. (5) and (6) consumer price index number of industrial workers.

Appendix 3.2

Incremental Capital Output Ratio and Growth Rates of Net National Domestic Product during the Five Year Plans

Period	Incremental capital output ratio	Growth rate of net national domestic product
First Five Year Plan	2.87	3.5
Second Five Year Plan	3.56	4.0
Third Five Year Plan	6.13	2.6
Fourth Five Year Plan	4.79	3.2
Fifth Five Year Plan	3.36	4.8
Seventh Five Year Plan	2.72	5.6
Sixth Five Year Plan	2.74	5.5
Average	3.70	4.0

Source : Prasad K.N., *Indian Economy Since 1951. Growth with Imbalances*, Intellectual Publishing House, New Delhi, 1993, pp. 409 and 411.

Appendix 3.3

Annual Rate of Population Growth

Year	Percentage
1951-61	2.0
1961-71	2.2
1971-81	2.2
1981-91	2.1
1951-91	2.2

Source : *Centre for Monitoring Indian Economy, Basic Statistics : States, Monthly Review of the Indian Economy,* Economic Intelligence Services, Bombay, September, 1994, table 1.1.

Appendix 3.4

Percentage of Private and Public Investment during the Five Year Plans

	Private Investment	Public Investment
First Five Year Plan	53.6	46.4
Second Five Year Plan	45.4	54.6
Third Five Year Plan	36.3	63.7
Fourth Five Year Plan	39.7	60.3
Fifth Five Year Plan	42.4	57.6
Seventh Five Year Plan	47.1	52.9
Sixth Five Year Plan	52.2	47.8
Average	45.0	54.7

Source : Prasad, K.N. : *Indian Economy Since 1951 : Growth with Imbalances*, Intellectual Publishing House, 1993, p. 88.

Appendix 4.1

The Working of the Two Schemes is explained with reference to Punjab in Part A and extended to all the States in Part B (Restructuring of NFC)

(Rs. Crores)

Part A	
The minimum additional plan revenue expenditure required	926
The available resources for revenue plan financing under 'NFC' scheme	834
1. Plan revenue grant on Gadgil basis	258
2. 40 per cent post-devolution surplus	576
Budgetary position under 'NFC' scheme (deficit)	-92
Five per cent covered by awarding plan deficit grant	46
Punjab will still have a deficit 'NFC' scheme	-46
The available resources for revenue plan financing under 'AS'	1658
1. Plan revenue grant on Gadgil basis	258
2. 100 per cent post-devolution surplus	1400
Budgetary position under 'AS' (surplus)	732
Plan deficit grant awarded under 'NFC' scheme	46
Budgetary position after plan deficit grant (surplus)	778
Part B	
Restructuring the 'NFC' scheme on 'AS' basis will release resources from group 2 and group 3 States to be allocated to group 4 States to meet their 100 per cent plan revenue deficit (instead of 50 per cent) The resources required to meet 100 per cent plan revenue deficit of group 4 States	8803
50 per cent already provided by plan deficit grant by 'NFC' scheme	4401.5
Resources released from group 2 States (Punjab, Tamil Nadu, Andhra Pradesh) Col.(8) 50 per cent plan deficit grant awarded to them).	431
Resources released from group 3 States (West Bengal, Kerala, Bihar and Madhya Pradesh reduced plan revenue deficit under 'AS' requiring reduced plan deficit grant)	1616
Plan revenue deficit 'NFC' scheme- Rs. 7667 crores. 50 per cent plan revenue deficit grant under 'NFC'	3833.5
Reduced plan revenue deficit under 'AS'- Rs. 4435 crores 50 per cent plan revenue deficit grant required under 'AS'	2217.5
The resources released under 'AS' and available for meeting 100 per cent plan deficit of group 4 States.	6448.5
Uncovered gap under 'AS'	2354.5
Uncovered gap under 'NFC' scheme	8666

Appendix 4.2

Per Capita Transfers Recommended by the Second to Eighth Finance Commissions

(Rs.)

States	Second Finance Commissi-ion	Third Finance Commissi-ion	Fourth Finance Commiss-ion	Fifth Finance Commiss-ion	Sixth Finance Commiss-ion	Seventh Finance Commiss-ion	Eighth Finance Commiss-ion	Aggregate per capita transfer
Gujarat	18.52	38.70	29.82	86.45	122.07	282.66	436.67	952.23
Haryana	-	-	22.34	75.27	105.84	239.20	640.48	747.67
Maharashtra	29.26	28.39	33.60	96.59	126.61	272.94	419.65	944.97
Punjab	29.83	29.23	28.64	83.21	111.90	249.72	384.61	891.37
Tamil Nadu	22.31	26.27	33.39	90.00	120.76	310.66	509.28	1067.69
West Bengal	21.84	24.95	28.58	101.34	167.26	292.51	631.86	1215.08
Andhra Pradesh	25.92	32.23	34.58	94.89	161.00	284.58	541.41	1114.11
Karnataka	32.83	32.40	47.56	84.40	115.25	270.89	465.76	983.60
Kerala	23.51	38.07	57.33	109.29	206.00	302.09	505.20	1173.09
Bihar	21.56	20.73	22.19	90.20	134.51	316.58	603.79	1159.56
Madhya Pradesh	23.68	25.29	25.79	82.28	116.42	306.03	506.61	1091.56
Orissa	28.55	54.20	68.54	131.22	239.55	372.00	723.35	1533.13
Rajasthan	25.49	32.32	32.34	102.73	189.23	263.21	488.68	1051.04
Uttar Pradesh	19.86	19.01	25.56	87.48	136.27	298.89	550.50	1087.21

Source : Sastry M.L. and G.R. Reddy : *Centre-State Financial Relations*, Centre for Economic and Social Studies, Hyderabad, Concept Publishing Company, New Delhi, 1988, p. 144.

Appendix 4.3

Per Capita Tax Shares and Per Capita Grants from Second Five Year Plan to Sixth Five Year Plan

(RS.)

States	Second Five Year Plan		Third Five Year Plan		Annual Plans		Fourth Five Year Plan		Fifth Five Year Plan		Sixth Five Year Plan		Aggregate	
1	2		3		4		5		6		7		8	
	Tax	Grant	Tax	Grant	Tax	Grant	Tax	Grant	Tax	Grant	Tax	Grant	Tax	Grant
1. Gujarat	29	-	40	10	36	-	85	01	158	02	104	-	453	13
2. Haryana	19	05	32	01	33	-	72	-	138	-	89	-	383	06
3. Maharashtra	22	-	34	-	40	-	96	03	164	-	102	-	458	03
4. Punjab	19	05	32	01	31	-	82	-	144	-	91	-	399	06
5. Tamil Nadu	20	-	28	04	31	06	83	06	154	Neg.	114	Neg.	430	16
6. West Bengal	27	08	32	01	34	-	85	16	155	60	105	01	438	86
7. Andhra Pradesh	19	05	28	11	28	11	79	16	153	50	103	01	410	94
8. Karnataka	19	12	27	14	29	26	78	06	153	-	101	-	407	58
9. Kerala	18	05	30	15	30	37	86	24	149	104	113	Neg.	426	185
10. Bihar	16	04	25	02	26	-	87	01	153	25	116	01	423	33
11. Madhya Pradesh	17	07	27	05	28	02	81	02	152	-	109	-	414	14
12. Orrisa	18	10	31	33	30	50	82	51	145	114	114	30	420	288
13. Rajasthan	18	06	28	12	29	10	81	21	151	100	96	01	403	150
14. Uttar Pradesh	19	-	24	-	27	04	86	-	151	25	107	03	414	32

Source : George, K.K. " Statutory Transfers and inter-State Disparities", Sinha, R.K. edit. *Centre State Financial Relations in India*, Deep and Deep Publication, New Delhi, p. 273.

Note : Neg. stands for Negligible.

Appendix 4.4

Per Capita Tax Shares and Per Capita Grants and Total Transfers Recommended by Tenth Finance Commission (1995-96 to 1990-2000)

(Rs.)

States	Per capita tax shares	Per capita grants	Per capita total transfers
1	2	3	4
1. Gujarat	1890.33	203.07	2093.40
2. Haryana	1511.83	140.83	1652.66
3. Maharastra	1575.98	104.04	1680.02
4. Punjab	1519.23	206.25	1725.48
5. Tamil Nadu	2218.45	129.70	2516.32
6. West Bengal	2003.55	124.43	2272.02
7. Andhra Pradesh	2379.88	255.83	2358.45
8. Karnataka	2172.08	105.19	2037.88
9. Kerala	2438.18	170.61	2515.20
10. Bihar	2609.41	151.51	2731.24
11. Madhya Pradesh	2223.58	119.07	2446.14
12. Orissa	2710.80	284.88	3524.38
13. Rajasthan	2248.90	251.32	2844.52
14. Uttar Pradesh	2326.65	182.65	2538.31

Source : Bagche Amaresh : "Tenets of Tenth Finance Commission : A Critique", *Economic and Political Weekly*, August 5-12, 1995, p. 1988.

Appendix 5.1

Percentage Transfer of Financial Resources Through Various Agencies (1951-52 through 1984-85)

Agencies	First five year plan	Second five year plan	Third five year plan	Annual plan	Fourth five year plan	Fifth five year plan	Sixth five year plan
1	2	3	4	5	6	7	8
Finance Commission	31.2	32.0	28.4	33.3	35.9	43.1	38.4
Planning Commission	61.5	36.9	48.9	35.8	31.3	41.2	41.1
Others	7.3	31.1	22.7	30.8	32.8	15.7	20.5

Source : Sastry, M.L. and G.R. Reddy : *Center State Financial_Relations*, Center for Economic and Social Studies, Hyderabad and Concept Publishing Company, New Delhi, 1998, p. 13.

BIBLIOGRAPHY

Aggarwal, P.P., *The System of Grants-in-aid in India.* Asia Publishing House, Bombay, 1959 and 1965.

Ashok Mitra, "Levels of Regional Development in India, Census of India 1961, para IA(1)" as quoted in Hemlata Rao : *Regional Disparities and Development in India.* Ashish Publishing House, New Delhi, 1984.

Bagchi Amaresh : "Ninth Finance Commission's Award II : Some Central Issues", *Economic and Political Weekly,* June 9,1990.

Bagchi Amaresh : "Tenets of Tenth Finance Commission : A Critique", *Economic and Political Weekly,* August 5-12, 1995.

Bajaj, J.L., Singh, K.S. and Aggarwal, O.P., *Finance Commission and Backward States.* Print House (India), Lucknow, 1985.

Baljit Singh, *Federal Finance and Underdeveloped Economy.* Hind Kitabs, Bombay, 1952.

Bauer, P.T. and Yomey, Basil, S., *The Economics of Underdeveloped Countries.* The University of Chicago Press, Chicago, 1957.

Bhargava, P.K., *Centre-State Resources Transfers in India.* Academic Press, Gurgaon, 1982.

Bhargava, R.N., *Indian Public Finances,* Orient Congmans. Bombay, Revised Edition, 1970.

Bhargava, R.N., *Theory and Working of Union Finance in India,* 3rd ed. Chaitanya Publishing House, Allahabad, 1971.

Bhatnagar, Sudha, *Union State Financial Relations and Finance Commission.* Allahabad, Chugh Publications, 1979.

Bombwall, K.R., *The Foundations of Indian Federalism.* Asia Publishing House, Bombay, 1967.

Bombwall, Raman, *Federal Financial Relations in India*. Meenakshi Prakashan, Meerut, 1970.

Boskey Shirley, *Problems and Practices of Development Banks*, Baltimore, The John Hopkins Press, 1959, as quoted by Prabhu N. Singh in *Role of Development Banks in A Planned Economy*. Vikas Publishing House Pvt. Ltd., Delhi, Bombay, Centre for Monitoring Indian Economy, Basic Statistics : States. *Monthly Review of the Indian Economy*. Published by Economic Intelligence Service, Bombay, September, 1994.

Chanada, Asok, *Federalism in India : A study of Union States Relations*. London, 1965.

Chatterji, Amiya, Central Financing of State Plans in the *Indian Federation*. Firma K.L. Mukhopadhyay, Calcutta, 1971.

Chelliah, Raja. J., *An Economic and Equity Aspect of the Distribution of Financial Resources Between the Centre and the State in India*. National Institute of Public Finance and Policy, 1983.

Chelliah Raja. J and Associates, *Trends and Issues in India Federal Finance*, 1981. National Institute of Public Finance, New Delhi. Dhawan, Prehalad, B., *Regional Needs and Financial Capacity*. Planning Commission, New Delhi. Diwan, Paras, *Union-State Fiscal Relations : An Overview*. Light and Life, New Delhi, 1981.

Datta Bhabatosh., Our Crumbling Federal Finance System : Seventh Finance Commission's Award. *Economic and Political Weekly*, January 13, 1979.

Forum of Free Enterprise, *Federal Financial Relations in India and other Essays*. A.D. Shroff Memorial Lectures, Lalwani Publishing House, New Delhi, 1967.

Gadgil, D.R., Planning and Economic Policy in India, (4th ed). Gokhala Institute of Politics and Economics, Bombay, 1972.

George, K.K., *Centre-State Financial Flows and Inter-State Disparities in India*. School of Management Studies, Cochin University, Cochin, 1982.

George, K.K., Gulati, I.S., Centre-State Resource Transfer, 1951-1984. *Economic and Political Weekly*, Feb. 16, 1985.

Goerge, K.K., Non-Statutory, Non-Plan Fiscal Transfers, 1956-76. *Economic Times*, June 22 and 23, 1978.

Government of India : *Report*, New Delhi, December, 1987. This report is commonly known as Sarkaria Commission Report (SCR) and in the present study also it has been referred to as such.

Government of India : *Report of the First Finance Commission*, 1952.

Government of India : *Report of the Second Finance Commission*, 1957.

Government of India : *Report of the Third Finance Commission*, 1961.

Government of India : *Report of the Fourth Finance Commission*, 1965.

Government of India : *Report of the Fifth Finance Commission*, 1969.

Government of India : *Report of the Sixth Finance Commission*, 1972.

Government of India : *Report of the Seventh Finance Commission*, 1978.

Government of India : *Report of the Eighth Finance Commission*, 1988.

Government of India : *First Report of the Ninth Finance Commission*, 1989.

Government of India : *Second Report of Ninth Finance Commission*, 1990.

Government of India : *Report of the Tenth Finance Commission*, 1995.

Government of India : *Report of the Eleventh Finance Commission*, 2000.

Grewal B.S. : *Centre-State Financial Relations in India*. Punjabi University, Patiala, 1975.

Guhan, S., Ninth Finance Commissions : Flawed Devolution Scheme. *Economic and Political Weekly*, June 9, 1990.

Guhan, S. "Report of Tenth Finance Commission", *Economic and Political Weekly*, April 22, 1995.

Gulati I.S. and George K.K. "Inter-State Redistribution Through Institutional Finance", *Economic and Political Weekly*, August 1978.

Gulati, I.S. "Sixth Finance Commission award", *Economic and Political Weekly*, Bombay, February 1977.

Gulati, I.S. and George, K.K., Inter-State Redistribution Through Budgetary Transfers. *Economic and Political Weekly*, March 11, 1978.

Gulati, I.S., Sixth Finance Commission's Award : An Appraisal in Retrospect. *Economic and Political Weekly*, July 30, 1977.

Gupta, R.N., *Indian Federal Finance and Budgetary Policy*. Chaitanya Publishing House, Allahabad, 1970.

Hanson, A.H. *The process of Planning*, Oxford University Press, London, 1966.

Hicks, U.K. and others (ed.). *Federalism and Economic Growth in Underdeveloped Countreiss*. London, 1961.

Jha, Prabodh Kumar, *Federal Finance in Developing India*. Capital Publishing House, 1983.

Joshi, M.D. (ed.), *Mobilisation of State Resources*, Impex India. New Delhi, 1967.

Kashyap, S.C., *Union-State Relations in India*. I.C.P.S., New Delhi, 1969.

Lakdawala, D.T., Ninth Finance Commission's Award I : An Overview. *Economic and Political Weekly*, June 9, 1990.

Lakdawala, D.T., *Union-State Financial Relations*. Lalvani Publishing House, Bombay, 1967.

M. Govinda Rao, Ninth Finance Commission : Some Conceptual and Methodological Comments. *Economic and Political Weekly*, June 9, 1990.

M. Govinda Rao, R.T., Shand K.P. Kalirajan, *Economic and Political Weekly*, September 16, 1995.

Morris D,. "*Measuring The Conditions of The World* Poor". The Physical Quality of Life Index, Overseas Development Council, Peragamon Press, New York, 1979.

Musgrave, Richard, A., *The Theory of Public Finance.* Kogakusha Company Ltd., Tokyo, 1959.

Musgrave, Richard A. (ed.), *Essays in Fiscal Federalism.* Brookings Institution, Washington, D.C., 1967.

Myrdal, Gunnar, *Economic Theory and Underdeveloped Regions.* Vora and Co. Publishers Pvt. Ltd., Indian Edition, Bombay, 1958.

Nambiar, K.V., Equity, Development and Federal Finance — Review Article. *Economic and Political Weekly,* June 12, 1982.

Nambiar, K.V., Role of the Finance Commission in Correlating *Inter-State Disparities in Essential Public Services.* Economic Science, Tala Consultancy Services, December, 1982.

Nanjudappa, D.M., *Inter-Governmental Financial Relations in India.* Sterling Publishers, New Delhi, 1974.

National Bureau of Economic Research, Public Finances, Needs, Sources and Utilization. Princeton, Princeton University Press, 1961.

National Institute of Public Finance and Policy, *Trends and issues in Indian Federal Finance.* Allied Publishers, New Delhi, 1981.

Nurkse, R., *Problems of Capital Formation in Underdeveloped Countries.* Delhi : Oxford University Press, 1973, India (reprint).

Phul Chand (Ed.), *Federal Financial Relations in India.* The Institute of Constitutional and Parliamentary Studies, New Delhi, 1974.

Planning Commission Report : *On Estimation of Proportion and Number of Poor,* July, 1993.

Prabhu N. Singh : *Role of Development Banks in A Planned Economy.* Vikas Publishing House Pvt. Ltd., Delhi, 1974, p. 63.

Rao, Hemlata, *Regional Disparities and Development in India.* Ashish Publishing House, New Delhi, 1984.

Rao Hemlata : Federal Fiscal Trasfers : Objectives and Criteria. In, Sinha, R.K. (Ed.) *Central State Financial Relations in India,* Deep and Deep Publications, New Delhi, 1986.

Rao, Hemlata, *Centre-State Financial Relations.* Allied Publishers, New Delhi, 1981.

Renuka Viswanathan, Enforcing Fiscal Discipline. *Economic and Political Weekly,* June 9, 1990.

Reserve Bank of India : *Report of the Tenth Finance Commission-* A Summary, Reserve Bank of India Bulletin, Jan-February, 1996.

Santhanam, K., *Federal Financial Relations in India.* Forum of Free Enterprises, Bombay, 1966.

Sarkar, P.C. : "Regional imbalances in Indian Economy Over Plan Periods", *Economic and Political Weekly,* March 12, 1994.

Sastri, K.V.S., *Federal-State Fiscal Relations in India, A study of the Finance Commission and the Techniques of Fiscal Adjustment.* Oxford University Press, Bombay, 1966.

Sastry, M.L. and G.R. Reddy, : *Centre-State Financial Relations.* Centre for Economic and Social Studies, Hyderabad and Concept Publishing Company, New Delhi, 1988.

Sharma, J.N., *Union and the States : A study in Fiscal Federalism.* Sterling Publishers. New Delhi, 1971 and 1974.

Singh, Shailendra (ed.), *Union-State Financial Relations in India : with Special Reference to the Underdeveloped States.* Sterling Publishers, New Delhi, 1977.

Singh, Prabhu, N., *Role of Development Banks in Planned Economy.* Vikas Publishing House Pvt. Ltd., Delhi, 1974.

Sinha R.K., *Centre-State Finance Relation.* Deep and Deep Publications, New Delhi, 1986.

Thakur Ramanand, *Finance Commissions and Centre-State Relation in India.* Deep and Deep Publications, New Delhi, 1982 and 1989.

Thimmaiah, G., *A critique of the Finance Commission.* Wheeler Publishing, New Delhi, 1981.

Thimmaiah, G., *Burning issues in Centre-State Financial Relations.* Ashish Publishing House, New Delhi, 1985.

Thimmaiah, G. and Hemlata Rao : *Finance Commission and Centre State Financial Relations.* Ashish publishing House, New Delhi, 1986.

Thammaiah, G., 'Second Report of the Ninth Finance Commission : Manipulated Normative Approach'. In Shandilya (Ed.) *Centre-State Financial Relations in India.* Deep and Deep Publications, New Delhi, 1994.

Tripathi, R.N., *Federal Finance in a Developing Economy.* World Press, Calcutta, 1960.

Tripathi, R.N., *Fiscal Policy and Economic Development in India,* 2nd. ed. World Press, Calcutta, 1970.

Uma Datta Roy Choudhury : "Inter-State and Intra-State variations in Economic Development and Standard of living". *Economic and Political weekly,* December 5-12, 1992.

Veeraraghavachar, S.M., *Union-State Financial Relations in India.* Sterling Publishers, New Delhi, 1969.

Venkataraman, K., *State Finances in India.* George Allen and Unwin, London, 1968.

Wheare, K.C., *Federal Government,* Third Edition. Oxford University Press, London, 1953.